The
World
of Mike

Royko

Doug
Moe

Introduction by

John
Kass

The University of Wisconsin Press

The University of Wisconsin Press
2537 Daniels Street
Madison, Wisconsin 53718

3 Henrietta Street
London WC2E 8LU, England

Printed in Canada

Library of Congress Cataloging-in-
 Publication Data
Moe, Doug.
 The world of Mike Royko/Doug Moe.
  pp. 128   cm.
  Includes bibliographical references
   (p. 113).
  ISBN 0-299-16540-X (alk. paper)
  1. Royko, Mike 1933–1997.
  2. Journalism—Illinois—Chicago—
  History—20th century. 3. Journalists—
  United States—Biography. 4. Chicago
  (Ill.)—Biography. I. Title.
  PN4874.R744 M64   1999
  070.92—dc21   99-6586
  [B]

Opposite **Mike and Bob Royko**

For Bob Royko

Acknowledgments

This book grew out of a lunch I had with Bob Royko, Mike's brother, in Madison, Wisconsin, where we both live, early in 1998. I must first of all thank Bob and his wife, Geri, for their many kindnesses. Our families have become good friends in the process of doing this book, and it is a friendship I value greatly.

On a strictly professional level, Bob did many of the original interviews on which this book is largely based. He began a few months after Mike's death in April 1997 and continued until the summer of 1998, when he passed the baton to me. He knew the importance of his brother's life and work and wanted to record it. I have no doubt that it wasn't always easy for Bob, so soon after Mike's death, but he was engaged in a labor of love. Everyone should have such a brother.

Mike's sisters, Eleanor Cronin and Dorothy Zetlmeier, who still live in the Chicago area, were interviewed and provided invaluable family photos. The same is true of Mike's two oldest sons, David Royko and Rob Royko. David also gave permission to quote from letters Mike sent from Washington State to Chicago while he was courting Carol Duckman, who became his wife and the boys' mother. In addition, David made available the original manuscript of *Boss,* complete with Mike's cross-outs and corrections. My thanks to them all.

Judy Royko, Mike's widow, supplied photos and graciously invited me into her home for an interview. I greatly appreciate her kindness and know this book is richer for it.

Mike's friend and colleague Rick Kogan helped by being interviewed, by reading and commenting on the manuscript, and by picking up a substantial bar tab at the Intercontinental Hotel on Michigan Avenue.

Hanke Gratteau, Mike's trusted friend and assistant at three different papers, was extremely helpful from the project's inception. No wonder Mike sought Hanke out when the chips were down, including asking her to come back as his leg person when he made the difficult move from the *Sun-Times* to the *Tribune*. Hanke sat for a formal interview but also served as the book's point person in Chicago, helping with a variety of logistical concerns, much of it while in the early weeks of a prestigious new job at the *Tribune*.

Don Karaiskos, Mike's friend from the air force, consented to an interview as did three close friends of later vintage: Sam Sianis, proprietor of the Billy Goat Tavern, John Sciackitano, a newspaper and softball buddy, and Dan Hurley, a contractor and golf partner.

My friend Jeff Scott Olson, a Madison attorney and gifted photographer, made more than one trip to Chicago, and his photos are a great asset to the book. Thanks also to Madison attorney Tim Sweeney for his help with contractual fine print.

I mentioned that Hanke Gratteau was our point person in Chicago. That job in Madison fell to Joan Strasbaugh at the University of Wisconsin Press. Her tasks included the sometimes impossible chore of getting busy newspaper people to return phone calls, and Joan handled it all with unfailing good humor.

Mike Royko did not particularly enjoy giving interviews, but he gave several I have drawn on, and those that appeared in newspapers and magazines are included in the bibliography. My favorite of the print profiles, and the one I drew on the most, was the first full-blown national magazine piece on Mike—William Brashler's "The Man Who Owns Chicago," published in *Esquire* in May of 1979.

The two most extensive interviews ever conducted with Royko were broadcast interviews in the 1990s: one with Chris Robling of WBEZ-FM radio in Chicago on the thirtieth anniversary of Royko's first column, and another with Chicago's Towers Productions, which was producing a program on the first 150 years of the *Tribune*. I'd like to thank WBEZ and Towers Productions for their permission to quote from those interviews. I'd also like to thank the *Chicago Tribune* for permission to reprint a Royko column, as well as the *Chicago Sun-Times* for permission to print excerpts from several Royko columns that first appeared either in the *Sun-Times* or in the now defunct *Chicago Daily News* and for permission to reprint one full column from each of those papers.

Soon after he retires, the great Cal Ripken, the all-star third baseman for the Baltimore Orioles, will enter the Baseball Hall of Fame with the most astounding record in professional sports.

That's because for sixteen straight seasons, he played in 2,632 consecutive games.

He played when his legs had spring and when he felt like a dry weed out there. What amazed other big league players was his brilliant consistency.

But with all due respect to Ripken, I knew somebody who made him look weak.

His name was Mike Royko.

Those of us who were born in Chicago and loved newspapers and great writing were lucky to have him. He was the best newspaper columnist in America. When he died, second place wasn't even close.

Mike grew up in the neighborhoods and understood us. He spoke our language. He never talked down to people, he didn't use French words, and most important, he didn't suck up to power.

He told stories as tough as Chicago and as sentimental as Chicago, reflecting the common sense of the people of Chicago.

Simply put, Mike was Chicago. And almost every day, you'd hear that phrase, at a coffee shop or at a bar or on the bus or in the break rooms at factories and offices. Somebody would say, "Ju read Royko taday?"

What is astonishing is that he did it for more than thirty years. He wrote five columns a week. Nobody wrapped his ankles or pitched him batting practice. Toward the end, Royko cut down his work load to four a week. But when he felt like it, he'd do five.

During those thirty-plus years, he wrote about eight thousand columns.

Readers figured that since the columns were easy to read, they must have been easy to write. Since most weren't writers, they couldn't know. What's easy is bad writing. All you have to do is blurt on the typewriter.

Mike didn't blurt. Instead, he bled alone, slowly, over every word. And because he bled, he made something valuable. So he was awarded the most important award in American journalism.

It's not the Pulitzer Prize, which Royko won, or the many other official journalism tributes. The important award is the Refrigerator Prize. We readers cut out Mike's columns and put them on our refrigerators, at home and in workplace lunchrooms, for everyone to see.

After writing his column, he'd walk down to the Billy Goat Tavern, see his buddy Sam Sianis, and have a drink.

Then that clock inside him would start again. That empty space in the paper would start calling, demanding his attention. His friends, like Studs Terkel, said he rode a demon. They were right.

You write four columns each week, the demon comes as part of the deal. It's a partnership. The demon becomes your friend and your enemy. You created him because you needed him. But he gets hungry quick.

Mike Royko wrote his first column when I was a little boy, on September 6, 1963. Our teachers would bring his columns to school, and we'd talk about them in class,

especially when Chicago was showing an ugly bigoted face and Mike was encouraging people to drop the bricks.

He wrote his last column on March 21, 1997. By then I was grown, with my own kids, working at the *Chicago Tribune,* covering politics, lucky to stop in at his office and talk.

I remember the 1980 election for Cook County state's attorney. Young Richard Daley had to win to stay alive in politics. Royko bedeviled Daley's father, the late Mayor Richard J. Daley. But he decided to help the son.

In a series of columns just before the election, Royko peeled the skin from the Republican incumbent, Bernard Carey. The election was decided by fewer than 15,000 votes in Cook County. Royko carried Richie Daley.

Without Royko, Daley would have disappeared. So he would never have succeeded his father at City Hall. And the Daley family knows it. After Young Richie became the powerful mayor and boss of Chicago, Mike wrote a column that made some folks extremely angry. It wasn't his best column. He had the temerity to say that Mexico was a politically corrupt narco state, which was later proven true.

So thousands of angry Latino Americans protested outside the Tribune Tower. Liberals demanded his job, conveniently forgetting what Royko had done over a career committed to civil rights and civil liberties and fighting the bullies and the bigots when it counted. That day I covered a Daley news conference. The mayor surrounded himself with friendly Latino politicians for the cameras. So I asked Daley if—given the angry protests—he felt a debt of loyalty to Mike for that 1980 campaign.

"You should never offend anybody," Daley said, showing his true face in public.

Later, I told Mike about it in his office. He was hurt. He leaned back, lit a cigarette, and stared out the window. We talked about the sixties, when he was a target of the racists, when the liberals who were calling for his job were running to him for protection.

"Yeah, but they don't remember that, do they?" he said.

You could see his heart breaking. Like the demon, betrayal is part of the deal too. The job of writing a newspaper column is the best job in the world. But if you don't cheat and you love it, your heart will be broken. It's the way of things.

Now I'm in the space on page three of the *Tribune* where Mike was for so many years. I hope Mike would be proud.

But proud or not, I respect him for what he did and what he gave up to do it. The reason I wrote this introduction is that Bob Royko, Mike's brother, asked me.

We talked the other day about the dedication Mike put in his book *Boss,* the classic treatment of big-city politics. The dedication was for his sons, Robby and David, "and all the Sundays missed."

"That's what he gave up to do his job," Bob Royko said. "That's what you're giving up too. I hope you understand, and I hope you can make people understand."

I hope so too.

The World of Mike **Royko**

...ould ask for their

I'm sure that if somebo...

suburbs with plans to li...

bring in about 30,000 pote...

evening of entertainment,

have something to say abo...

So what's good for somebo...

. Cashflow Estates ought b...

her side of the right field...

s for those occasional men...

en that without lights...

ndoned and the...

forget...

1

"Flat-above-a-Tavern" Youth

This was 1955 and the United States Air Force was about to create a monster.

The young man's name was Royko, and he was from Chicago. He was tall, with a big nose and gravel voice, and he'd been transferred from a base in Washington State to O'Hare Field because his mother was very ill. He'd been a radio operator overseas during the Korean War, but the fighting had ended and at O'Hare they needed military policemen, not radio operators.

"They were going to make me a cop," he recalled later, and that meant having his shoes shined and walking around with an attitude and harassing people. Growing up in Chicago, the young Royko had been around cops. If they weren't chasing him, he was passing them an envelope full of cash across his dad's bar. He hemmed a bit.

Well, the personnel officer asked, what else?

Before coming to O'Hare, Royko had been stationed in Blaine, Washington, and one day, fooling around with a mimeograph machine, he began a little newspaper. He started with sports. Royko's roommate, Don Karaiskos, played on the base softball team, which, as Royko told his readers, meant he generally had to do a complete 360 just to throw a ground ball to first base. "Blaine Air Force Base," Royko wrote, "fields the only left-handed Greek shortstop in existence."

Several months later, talking with the personnel officer at O'Hare, Royko did what he had done so often as a kid growing up in taverns, taking bets and pouring drinks before he was fifteen. He lied.

"I worked as a reporter for the *Chicago Daily News*."

With that, Royko was named editor of the base newspaper, an eight-page weekly called the *O'Hare News*.

"I was a buck sergeant," he said later. "I had a Latvian immigrant private as my assistant, and the fact I could speak English gave me a big leg up on him." What Royko really knew of newspapers, which wasn't much, he'd picked up at the taverns, where there were always papers lying on the bar. He liked the sports columnists and a young gossip columnist named Irv Kupcinet. "I liked Kup. He was always writing about Bob Hope or somebody."

Now at O'Hare he was an editor. "I asked for a three-day pass and told them I was married and wanted to settle into my apartment. Actually I was already settled but I wanted to go to the library and check out some journalistic books."

He checked out one on reporting and one on prize-winning layouts, and the next week the *O'Hare News* carried the same front-page layout for which the *Kansas City Star* had once been greatly honored. The base was abuzz. What a fine change in the paper. But then, as editors will often do, young Royko rewarded himself with a column, "Mike's View." His first effort poked fun at the American Legion for its support of Joseph McCarthy, and it may have raised a few eyebrows. It was Royko's second column, though, that showed him "how fun journalism could be."

Royko pointed out that it was hardly fair that he and his service mates had to dress up and look presentable when the same wasn't

true of the wives of officers. "Officers' wives," he observed, "come on the base and go to the PX in dumpy house dresses, their hair in curlers, really looking awful."

On the day that issue hit the base several women barged into the newspaper office and demanded to know where they could find Airman Royko.

"He's on leave," the editor—Royko—said. "A thirty-day pass. He'll be back in twenty-nine days." When they left, Royko had to admit he enjoyed the reaction. "What power. You could write five hundred words and get people all excited." He loved the idea of the wives welcoming their officer husbands home by shaking a copy of the *O'Hare News* at them and yelling, "Mike Royko? Who's Mike Royko?"

Mike Royko (left) and a couple of air force buddies in the early 1950s. Royko got his start in journalism working on base newspapers.

One of the best-known names in
American journalism, Royko was a
living legend in Chicago, invaluable
for selling newspapers.

Before too long, the world would know. At the time of his death in 1997, Mike Royko was one of the best-known names in American journalism, a best-selling author, a daily columnist many believed to be the best ever to attempt that grueling exercise, syndicated in over six hundred papers around the world, winner of the Pulitzer Prize for commentary, a controversial, fearless Chicago legend.

When President George Bush was campaigning for reelection in 1992, he stopped at the Billy Goat Tavern, a shot-and-beer joint located below Michigan Avenue in the heart of downtown Chicago. Bush was hoping to have a beer with Mike Royko, the bar's most celebrated customer. The bar people called Royko's wife and his assistant at the *Chicago Tribune,* frantic to find him, but when they did, the columnist said he had better things to do. He was watching the rape trial of a Kennedy kid on television. The truth was he didn't feel like joining Bush's entourage for a photo opportunity. Royko had his faults, and they would occasionally be on public display over the years, but social climbing or breaking bread with a president for an ego massage was not among them. Of course, he got a column out of it. When you write five columns a week, as Royko did for most of his career, you find columns where you can.

Many of Royko's best columns were informed by his upbringing, which, while unconventional, provided a wealth of material, perfect for the blunt humor that became his sword as a writer.

His forebears had had little to laugh about. Royko's father, Michael Royko—no middle name—was born in a field in the town of Dolina, part of the Russian Ukraine near the Czech border, in 1895. "I was picking potatoes in the field and he decided to be born," said Michael's mother, Anna Wolkowski. "I picked him up and I cut the cord and I did what I had to do. I put him in the apron and took him in the house. I made sure he was okay and I put him back in my apron and went out and finished picking potatoes."

Michael's father, George Royko, had met Anna in Dolina, a lumber town where George was a night watchman at the lumber mill. The family didn't have much to start with. Then when Michael was five there was a fire at the mill, and George, in the bitter cold, ran to battle the fire, saving what he could but contracting a pneumonia that eventually killed him. Anna, Michael, and his two sisters stayed with Anna's sister, who had twelve children of her own. The Royko kids ate in the barn. There was never enough food.

Desperate, Anna brought the children to the United

States. Eventually the family found its way to Chicago, where Anna had a brother who got her a job in a laundry.

One night when Michael Royko was in the his early twenties, at a dance hall on Chicago's North Side, he went up to a girl in her late teens, whose name he later learned was Helen Zak, and said, "You know, you're not much of a dancer, but you're really a looker." It wasn't a great line, but they began dating and ended up marrying.

Helen—Mike Royko's mother—was the daughter of Anton Zak, a Russian immigrant, and Amelia Bielski, also an immigrant. Anton and Amelia had a farm in the United States near the turn of the century when Amelia, restless, convinced her husband they should return to Europe, where her family had some money. The stories that were passed down the generations disagree on whether Mike's mother was born on a ship going to Europe or on a ship headed for the United States. The latter is likely, since her birthplace is listed as New Jersey, and the custom was to list the destination as the place of birth.

Once Anton and Amelia returned to Europe, Amelia bought a hotel that housed a bakery and restaurant. Anton, though, soon wanted to return to the United States. That was fine with Amelia. Here is some money, she said. You go back, buy another farm. I'll sell everything here and join you.

Top **Anton Zak (right), father of Helen Zak, Mike Royko's mother.**

Bottom **Mike Royko's mother, Helen, about the time she met Mike's father at a Chicago dance hall.**

In fact, Amelia had no intention of going back at that time. They didn't divorce, but she never saw Anton Zak again. Instead Amelia met a handsome Russian army officer, and they fell in love. They decided to come to the United States, with the officer using Amelia's brother's passport and family name, Bielski. Helen and her siblings came with them, but Amelia and the Russian officer were drinkers and it wasn't long before they split up. Amelia was later killed by a hit-and-run driver as she walked from a theater on Milwaukee Avenue. Bielski ended up on skid row. When Mike Royko became famous as a columnist, he told an interviewer Bielski had been fatally stabbed in a bar fight. That wouldn't have been surprising, but no evidence exists to support the story. In any event, Helen Zak, her family life a shambles, was altogether ready to be swept off her feet when she met Michael Royko at the Chicago ballroom.

They married and quickly had two daughters, Eleanor in 1921 and Dorothy two years later. Michael worked a series of jobs. He was uneducated, though a doctor once told the family he had an unusually high IQ. But he couldn't read, at least not until he asked his daughter Eleanor to bring home grade-school books. "You're going to teach your father to read," he said, and Eleanor did.

Mike Royko's grandmother Anna (second from left), who gave birth to Royko's father while working in a field in the Russian Ukraine, and members of her extended family. Anna's left hand is on the shoulder of Mike Royko's sister Eleanor.

Mike Royko's immediate family, sans
Michael Sr. From left: Eleanor, Helen,
Bob, Mike, and Dorothy.

On September 19, 1932, in St. Mary of Nazareth Hospital at Division and Leavitt Streets on the near Northwest Side of Chicago, Michael Royko Jr. was born. At the time his father was working as a milkman for the Pure Farm Dairy.

"We never saw him," Dorothy said of her father. "He was always working. He went to bed early because he was a milkman and he was out of the house at two or three in the morning. He got the job by basically making his own route. He was very aggressive. He had almost two hundred customers and he knew how to do it. Give the Polish ladies some free butter and buttermilk. He knew how to do it." The family lived in a basement apartment near Wolcott and Division behind a store where Helen operated a cleaning and tailoring business. Anna, Michael Royko's mother, lived with them.

Years later, when the columnist Mike Royko became one of the most talked about people in the Midwest, his sisters thought it made perfect sense. From a very early age he commanded attention. They called him Mickey.

"I adored him," Eleanor said. "He was cute and he was smart. I was very proud of how smart he was. He loved to be read to. When he started talking, he was anxious to talk, anxious to learn. He was a real nice kid.

Top **Mike Royko, skinny as a kid but pretending otherwise.**

Bottom **Mike (back right), Bob (back middle), and a number of their cousins.**

He never cried. I don't remember him ever crying. I do remember that, by the time he was four, he knew he was in control. Tell him to do something, and he'd say, 'Where's Daddy?' 'Why do you need Daddy?' 'Well, I want to ask him.' "

By 1935 Mike had a baby brother, Bob, and the Roykos bought a tavern at 2122 North Milwaukee Avenue. It was called the Blue Sky Lounge because a supplier had given them a bunch of blue crepe paper with little stars that they stuck up to make an artificial ceiling. The family moved into the flat above the tavern, and Helen stacked boxes on the floor of the second-floor flat to make certain none of the children wandered onto the "blue sky." They never did, but one time an uncle, having been overserved downstairs, went up to the flat and promptly fell through the false ceiling. Mike Sr., standing behind the bar, shook his head and said, "He always was a dumb sonofabitch."

The tavern move was one of the best things and one of the worst things that ever happened to Mike Royko. Best, because the strange characters and funny lines and burlesque goings-on from those years were wonderful fodder for the daily columnist he became twenty-five years later. Worst, because with the move to the bar business, his father drank more and fought with his wife and abused her physically. They divorced. Mike had a front-row seat for that, and it was rough.

"The bar had a very disruptive effect on my mom and dad's relationship," Bob Royko says. "He was a heavy drinker, he gambled, he caroused, and under that circumstance, it was just a question of time. He was a very gregarious guy, always running dances, and apparently there were opportunities out there that he just had a difficult time rejecting, and so it was very disruptive on the marriage. And Mike was more of a witness to that than I was. He was a little older. They had some bad times together, and it definitely had a lasting effect on him."

But that wasn't what he later wrote about. When Royko wrote about those years, he did it through the eyes of his marvelous creation, Slats Grobnik, a "flat-above-a-tavern" youth who bore a remarkable similarity to his creator, right down to his skinny frame, big nose, and outsized feet—not to mention his social proclivities.

"There is my boyhood friend, Slats Grobnik," Royko wrote. "His parents took him with them on all their social outings, most of which were to the Happy Times Tavern on Armitage, which was owned by Slats' uncle, Beer Belly Frank Grobnik. . . . They would sit him on the bar or the pinball machine and he was the most contented child you ever saw, chewing on a hard-boiled egg, washing it down with a tiny tumbler of beer. . . . Customers enjoyed having Slats around and would bounce him on their knees and give him snacks, such as herring, pickled pigs' feet, pep-

peroni, and beer foam. By the time he was three the only way Mrs. Grobnik could persuade him to drink milk was to put it in a stein and say, 'Have a snort, little Slats.' "

When he became well known, Royko rarely granted interviews, and when he did, he never talked much about growing up. An exception occurred in an interview with Chicago's Towers Productions in the 1990s. During that talk, it became clear Royko's Slats stories were an exaggeration firmly grounded in truth. He spoke of his grandfather—Bielski, whom whiskey put down for the count—and his unique style of babysitting.

The opening of the second Blue Sky Lounge, on Armitage Avenue, in 1940. Leaning on the building (from right) Mike, Bob, Eleanor, Eleanor's daughter, Barbara, and Helen.

"He used to babysit when I was four or five," Royko recalled. "His idea of babysitting was, they had those bars on Division Street, and I'd sit up there and drink ginger ale and he'd drink whatever he drank. In those bars you didn't hear any English. This was the thirties. All those guys looked like Joe Stalin—big mustaches. In that neighborhood English was a minority language."

It was less so with the move in 1938 to the Blue Sky Lounge on Milwaukee Avenue. "That neighborhood was a bit of a mix," Royko said. "I would say a minority of the patrons in my dad's bar spoke Polish. But the Polish newspaper was on the bar—all the newspapers were on the bar, in those days. My father could speak Polish, Ukrainian, some Russian. Both my parents could."

It was, in any case, a neighborhood—the beginning of the end of an era of self-contained ethnic neighborhoods in Chicago. As Royko himself wrote years later in *Boss*, his 1971 best-selling biography of Richard J. Daley, "Chicago, until as late as the 1950s, was a place where people stayed put for a while, creating tightly knit neighborhoods, as small-townish as any village in the wheat fields. The neighborhood-towns were part of larger ethnic states. To the north of the Loop was Germany. To the northwest was Poland. To the west were Italy and Israel. To the southwest were Bohemia and Lithuania. And to the south was Ireland."

There were no border patrols and you didn't need a passport to cross from one neighborhood state to another, but as Royko observed, "You could always tell, even with your eyes closed, which state you were in by the odors of the food stores and the open kitchen windows, the sound of the foreign or familiar language, and by whether a stranger hit you in the head with a rock."

Royko's, of course, was the Polish Northwest Side. Recalling it years later, he said, "Our neighborhood was typical of most. You didn't need a car. You could walk to everything. That stands out in my mind more than anything. Everything you needed was within walking distance. Women did all their shopping—you had all the stores nearby. Food stores, the community department store. Movie theaters. I could walk to six or eight movie theaters. In general the people were very blue collar, very working class. We didn't have professional people living in the neighborhood. The doctors you went to, their offices might be there, but they lived somewhere fancy—the land beyond Logan Square."

Milwaukee Avenue cuts through Logan Square at Kedzie Boulevard, and as a kid Royko thought if he ever got rich, he'd buy a house on the other side of Logan Square. He didn't, but in 1990 he told an interviewer, "Now I have dreams about walking home through that area. I don't know what the hell they mean."

Left **Mike and Sparky, the dog that alerted Mike and his brother Bob to a fire in their flat, possibly saving their lives.**

He probably had more fun growing up in his own neighborhood. This was long before soccer moms and youth sports leagues with organizational charters more complex than the United Nations. Kids hung out, and in Humboldt Park, Royko's neighborhood, they hung around the schoolyard. His younger brother, Bob, said, "The schoolyard was a place of great fun for us."

The grammar school was Salmon Chase, which made the news late in 1998 when Illinois Congressman Henry Hyde read a letter from a Chase student during the impeachment hearings of President Bill Clinton. The Chase school was surrounded by a sprawling grass field. "That was the focal point," Mike said. "The softball games were played there. You always met over at the schoolyard. You played touch football, you played sixteen-inch softball."

Many years later, he drove a journalist by the school, leaned over an iron fence that surrounded it, and shook his head at the broken asphalt covering the yard. "What the hell do they have to pave everything for? You know, I once hit a home run that flew across the street and scattered the pigeons in the loft at the back of the house. The pigeon loft's gone."

Royko's love for baseball endured, however. The Chicago Cubs and sixteen-inch softball—a Chicago favorite, played with a large, soft ball and no gloves—were two of the great passions of his life. The Cubs won the National League pennant in 1938—no one dreamed they'd win only one more in Royko's lifetime, in 1945—and the following April, Royko's dad, having hit the daily double at the race track the day before, took his son to opening day at Wrigley Field. Mike was six years old and it was his first Cubs game. His dad brought along a couple of friends from the neighborhood, Dutch Louie and Shakey Tony. Because it was cold, the grownups also brought along another friend—Jim Beam.

As they entered Wrigley Field, a cop saw young Mike and walked over. "Shouldn't that kid be in school?"

Dutch Louie thought fast. "He stayed home sick."

The cop asked, "What's the problem?"

"Pneumonia."

While the cop chewed on that, they made their way to their seats. When a Cub named Phil Cavaretta came up, Shakey Tony was overcome with excitement. He and Cavaretta were both Italian and had gone to Lane Tech, and he'd once met a relative of Cavaretta's in a bar. Obviously they were great friends. Shakey Tony stood up and screamed, "Phil! It's me! Tony!" Alas, Cavaretta flied out. A fan nearby made the mistake of calling him a bum. Shakey Tony stood up and faced the man: "Hey, you want to die? Huh? You want to die?"

Young Mike Royko was enthralled from the first pitch. The Cubs leadoff man sent a line drive banging off the

Fans celebrated the Cubs clinching the 1938 National League
pennant by storming the field.

The following April, Mike Royko's
father took him to opening day—
his first Cubs game.

right field wall and threw himself into third base with a triple. "I was hooked," Royko said later. "From that moment I was a Cub fan. Little did I realize it was a curse."

It wasn't—not really. Not with all the great times he had in all the subsequent trips to Wrigley Field and the great columns he produced after witnessing one Cub inefficiency or another. Maybe the spectacle of Wrigley Field turned his head from school—reading the Slats Grobnik columns, you'd assume Mike was rarely in a classroom—but the truth is, for quite a while he was a good student.

"He was moved up several times," Bob Royko says. "He graduated from grammar school at age twelve. He was extremely bright."

Mike recalled, "Most of the [neighborhood] families were fairly stable and the kids studied in school. Kids worked hard in school." Later he would remember that about 90 percent of the teachers were Irish women. He had Mrs. O'Malley, Mrs. O'Brien, and one in particular who stuck in his mind named Mrs. Keenan. Not only was she a good teacher but as the sister-in-law of Frank Keenan, a Chicago politician who wound up as the Cook County assessor, Mrs. Keenan offered an early look at the spoils of political clout. "She used to pull up at school in a limousine," Royko said. "We had the only teacher in the Chicago Public Schools system who arrived at school in a limo."

She did not spoil her students, insisting they read Victor Hugo. "She was a tough little teacher. Our eighth grade project was to read *Les Misérables.* That was very good. I learned at a very early age if you're going to steal something, do better than a set of candelabras. Why spend your life on the run for something like that?"

If the young Royko was a good student, he was also reliable in a pinch. The first time their parents left Bob and Mike alone, the flat caught fire and only the barking of their dog, Sparky, woke them. Mike helped Bob outside and then, infuriating the firefighters who were just arriving, ran back inside through the smoke, found the dog hiding under the stove, grabbed it, and carried it outside, saving its life. Another time, when Mike was about twelve, his older sister Eleanor, with kids of her own, was fixing everyone a spaghetti lunch when she accidentally dumped a pot of scalding water on her hand. "I turned around and he was gone," Eleanor said. "I thought: 'That coward. Just when I need him he runs away.'"

In fact, he had run to a drugstore on the nearby corner of California and Armitage, asked for a burn remedy, and bought some ointment. When he came panting back a few minutes later, Eleanor thought, "God, how I've underestimated this kid."

He was also working—he was always working. Later, when people expressed amazement that he could keep

Right **The Royko clan. Back (left to right): Bob, Eleanor, and Dorothy; front: Helen, Mike, and Mike Sr.**

pounding out column after column, five a week for
months, years—more than eight thousand in all—Royko
would often shrug. It was a job. You did your job.

He had many jobs before most kids have one. He bartended at the Blue Sky Lounge and then, after his parents
divorced and his mother opened the Hawaiian Paradise
on Ashland Avenue, he bartended there, too. Royko later
recalled that these were not the kinds of places where bar-
tenders made a lot of ice cream drinks. His duties, he
wrote, were as follows: "Accepting bets on horses; pre-
venting customers from falling asleep with head in toilet;
admitting regular patrons through side door at 8:00 A.M.
on Sunday so they could get over the shakes and go to
church; answering phone and telling wives that husbands
had not been there all evening; appraising wristwatches
for payments of drinks in lieu of cash; dispensing hard-
boiled eggs, pickled pigs feet, beef jerky, and other gour-
met delights; breaking up fights by unleashing a Dober-
man named Death and letting him gnaw on brawlers
until peace was restored; and, finally, giving monthly
cash-stuffed envelopes to police bagman for assorted
favors, such as overlooking a thirteen-year-old bartender."

Royko also worked as a theater usher, a stock boy
at Marshall Field's, and—one of his more colorful occupa-
tions—a pinsetter at the Congress Bowling Alley. His
brother, Bob, also set pins. "It was an interesting educa-

Downtime in the air force in
Washington State.

tion," Bob said. "There were some winos back there and some real weirdos setting pins. But there was a lot of good music, and if you were good, you learned to grab two pins at a time and flip them in the rack."

This was the mid-forties. In 1968 Mike Royko was delighted to find, at Chicago Recreation on West Twenty-sixth Street, a creature "widely believed to be extinct"—a pinboy. "This is a discovery of which I am proud," Royko told his readers in the *Chicago Daily News*. "I feel like one of those scientists who creep around a swamp for years and then spot a rare bird."

He then explained why almost all bowling alleys had become automated—"most teenagers prefer to knock pins down rather than set them up"—and recalled his own pin-setting days. "The pay rate, as I recall, was about 7 or 8 cents a game. So if you set 'double' (adjoining alleys) for two leagues, you worked 60 games in about four or five hours and earned $4.80, plus maybe 50 cents or a dollar in tips. Pinsetting was also a fine physical fitness program. To earn the $4.80, you bent over about 2,000 times. There weren't too many fat pinboys. I don't know what the labor laws were, but many of us started setting pins when we were about 12. You could tell a pinboy by the joints on his first two fingers. Hoisting the pins between the fingers made them big."

Against this street education, the classroom paled.

Royko began not showing up. "He often said he was just horribly bored by school," Bob said. "And he was mouthy. I think there were problems with some of the bigger guys."

Spending more money than they could afford, Royko's parents enrolled him in the Morgan Park Military Academy on Chicago's far South Side, but he wasn't happy there. One time, however, after being hazed all week by a bunch of cadets who claimed Army would stomp Notre Dame in that weekend's featured college football game, Royko was delighted when Johnny Lujack made a tackle that saved a 0–0 tie for Notre Dame. "It was the only time at that place that I was happy, when Lujack made the tackle," he said. Bob would take the streetcar to see him a couple of times a month with a bag of fruit and candy their mother had packed. Royko lasted about a year at Morgan Park.

Chicago, like most cities, had a school for kids not yet sixteen—old enough to drop out—who kept getting in trouble. It was called Montefiore—Monty-fee for short—and it was where Royko ended up not long after he left the military academy. "It was one step away from jail," Bob Royko said. At Montefiore Royko made the acquaintance of one Angelo Boscarino. Boscarino looked like a fullback and distinguished himself at Monty-fee by losing a fight with a math teacher and then going berserk with a knife in biology class and filleting a live eel. Boscarino bailed from Monty-fee as soon as he turned sixteen and

It was there [O'Hare air base], of course, that to dodge being made a military cop, Royko claimed he had worked for the *Chicago Daily News* and was made editor of the base newspaper. "After three years in the service I knew they didn't check résumés. I was sent over to see the public information officer. That's when I realized I had taken a little chance. If he had just picked up the phone I suppose I would have had to plead insanity or something."

became a low-level organized crime figure. Royko followed Boscarino's career and later had the sad duty of informing his readers that Boscarino had died from what were, for Angie, natural causes—an ice pick in the throat. Police found him in a gutter on Chicago's West Side.

When Royko was old enough he dropped out—eventually earning his high school diploma from the Central YMCA downtown. That was Royko's kind of school—you could smoke in the halls, and one of the guys who voted for Mike when he ran successfully for class president had been a tailgunner during World War II. For prom they went to a neighborhood tavern and drank pitchers. He got his degree but he was drifting, working odd jobs, playing softball, occasionally showing up to watch his younger brother play high school basketball. Bob would see him in the stands, but Mike would leave before the game was over.

Mike had also developed an intense interest in Carol Duckman, a girl from the neighborhood who was three years younger than himself. Of course Mike was infatuated with her—everyone was. She was smart, blue-eyed, and blonde. Carol once fielded three marriage proposals in a week. She liked Mike—he could make her laugh like nobody else—but they were still very young. And the country was about to go to war in Korea.

"I think he enlisted because he didn't want to get drafted and go into the infantry," Bob Royko says of Mike's decision to enlist in the air force at the start of the Korean War. He was sent to Washington State and then to Korea. He wrote a lot of letters back home, but when he became a columnist, he rarely wrote about his time in Korea. When he did, it was usually in a light vein, as when he described how much it pained him to be involved in a feud with Frank Sinatra. "In 1953, I played his great record of 'Birth of the Blues' so often that a Korean houseboy learned all the words. And he probably taught the song to his children. So if Sinatra has a fan club in the Korean village of Yong Dong Po, it's because of me."

The truth is Royko was often in harm's way in Korea. When he returned to Blaine Air Force Base in Washington, he told his roommate, Don Karaiskos, a bit about his experiences. "He never talked about the war in philosophical terms," Karaiskos said. "But he was a forward air controller. I think that's what the title was. It was a rather hazardous thing. They would go out in front in a jeep and call in on the radio strikes from the air."

Karaiskos was the chief clerk at Blaine when the war ended, and all the records of the incoming personnel came across his desk. One day in the file of a returning airman Karaiskos saw something he had never seen before. "It was a score of 100, a perfect score, on his

Armed Forces Qualification Test. I thought, 'This guy's a brain. I want to meet him.' " He made a mental note of the name: Mike Royko.

Karaisko also worked some nights bartending at the Squadron Club. One night in the fall of 1953, about six weeks after spotting the exceptional test score, Karaiskos was getting ready to close the bar when someone he didn't recognize—which was unusual, since only about 150 men were stationed at Blaine—came in and said in a deep, husky voice, "What kind of beer you got?"

It was Royko. He introduced himself and ordered an Olympia. "I just got in," Royko said. "I guess I'll have to go up to Supply and find out where I'm going to bunk down."

Karaiskos, remembering the test, said, "My roommate was just discharged. You're welcome to move into my room if you want to."

They became very good friends. Throughout his life Royko gravitated toward people who were first- or second-generation immigrants, self-made, often rough hewn but never phony. At Blaine, the war over, they had a lot of fun together.

"He was extremely funny, very humorous," Karaiskos said. "We'd be sitting in the dining hall, which wasn't very big, and he'd get going and have us all in stitches. We were all laughing and the CO came over and told us to hold the noise down. That was him. I don't think he changed much from that."

Royko and Karaiskos got jobs tending bar at a golf course off the base, and they went in together on a car— a 1937 Graham-Paige that cost a hundred dollars. Royko became an accomplished golfer. For fifteen dollars you could play all summer and clubs were provided by Special Services on the base. At night, there were dates. Royko was seeing a Canadian woman named Daphne Snow. "She drove him crazy," Karaiskos said. "He'd come in after a date, two o'clock in the morning, and he's stomping around. She wanted a very platonic relationship and he was looking for a little more than that."

Much of the time his thoughts were of another female, the girl from his old neighborhood whom he first met when he was nine and she was six—Carol Duckman. "The thing that was uppermost in his mind was Carol," Karaiskos said.

When Royko went into the service Carol became involved with someone else, but it didn't last. Royko, once he was stationed at Blaine, went home for a brief visit and then wrote her prodigious, extraordinary letters, 115 in all between March and December of 1954. "I saw him write the letters," Karaiskos said. "We'd be going somewhere and he'd say, 'Let me finish this letter.' He'd be really deep in thought. I didn't realize at the time what a great writer he was, but those letters must have been extremely interesting."

One of the first letters Mike wrote to Carol, on March 16, 1954, showcased his humor. "It's great up here. They have weekly barn dances and during our time off we can chase rabbits or carve our names in Redwood trees. Nothing like a social life. The local farmers are very friendly, though. They probably reckon that I'll give 'em a mite of help with the spring plowin'. Needless to say, I left Korea somewhat gaunt but still intact. The first condition I attribute to the . . . dehydrated potatoes we lived on and the second to the fact that on guard duty, when sighting a Korean, I yelled 'help' instead of 'halt.' "

A month later he described an adventure with his car: "It provides me with laughs. Last week the horn decided to blow. I was on a quiet country road when it happened and it took five minutes for me to find the cause. While I was looking, the farmer whose sleep I had disturbed arrived on the scene, fully armed. He stood there yelling, 'Turn it off,' and his dog sat on the ground and barked. When I fixed the horn, he told me to git. I gitted."

In another letter Royko wrote: "I never cease to be amazed by the country out here. After living in Chicago and seeing the drabness of Korea, this mountainous country is fascinating. When I look out the window in the morning the mountains have a blue-white color. When

Royko wrote home often from his air force posts and looks happier in this photo than he probably felt. In one letter he said the air force promotions board had IQs ranging "from idiot to moron."

3.

and discovered that I've been spelling
marriage, "marraige." It seems Solomon &
those didn't fulfill its responsibility.

Lastic Sunday I'm taking a drive
to Mt. Baker. For the last three
months I've been looking out my window
and seeing this mountain and wondering
what it looks like close up so I've
made up my mind to find out. I'll
probably take a few pictures so if any of
them are worth seeing I'll send them. I never
cease to be amazed at the beauty of the
country around here. After living in Chicago
and then seeing the drab mess of Korea, this
mountainous country is fascinating. When
I look out the window in the morning,
the mountains have a blue white color. When
I was a kid, I'd look out the window
and see the blue white color of the Ralph
sign.

I was a kid I'd look out the window and see the blue-white color of the Pabst sign."

Still another letter made clear why Royko was never destined to ascend the ranks in the air force. Karaiskos says, "He hated the military—he hated taking orders." In the spring of 1954 Mike wrote Carol: "For two years I have been getting extra time off by conjuring some of the most fantastic excuses imaginable. This morning, my mind drew a blank so I did what everybody knows is the wrong thing to do. I told the truth. I told the woeful creature who is my boss that I wanted the morning off to write a letter. The ridiculousness of my request must have dulled his little brain because he said OK. That's twice in the last two days that I have told the truth in the so-called line of duty. Yesterday, it had the opposite effect. I met the promotions board (a group of men whose IQs ranged from idiot to moron, gathered together to determine whether my mind has become stagnant enough to assume the lofty title of 'sarge'), and I flunked with flying colors. I spent one whole hour answering questions correctly. . . . Finally, one sly little sergeant created my downfall. He asked me if I would order one of my friends to shine my shoes in the event that I was promoted. . . . I said 'no' quite emphatically. That ended the interview and also my chance for promotion this month. The results were posted and I was bypassed because of 'inability to assume responsibility.' "

Many of the letters were deeply romantic, and they won Carol over. In November 1954 she flew to Washington and they were married. Mike borrowed a more reliable car from somebody in the outfit, and they had a brief honeymoon before Carol returned to Chicago. A month or two later, Royko, citing the fact his mother in Chicago was very ill, requested and received a transfer to the air base at O'Hare.

It was there, of course, that to dodge being made a military cop, Royko claimed he had worked for the *Chicago Daily News* and was made editor of the base newspaper. "After three years in the service I knew they didn't check résumés. I was sent over to see the public information officer. That's when I realized I had taken a little chance. If he had just picked up the phone I suppose I would have had to plead insanity or something."

But that phone call was never made, and Mike Royko was a journalist. Not long after his column that so infuriated the officers' wives, Royko stumbled onto a scoop. With a big softball tournament coming up, Royko learned that the star pitcher's enlistment had been lengthened so he could play. Royko ran the story on page one, later claiming he just thought it was interesting. It was more than that—it was against the rules.

Left Mike and Carol Royko. Mike said he'd loved her since he was nine and she was six. He wrote over a hundred letters to Carol while courting her long distance during his air force days.

"The base adjutant who had arranged the extension was transferred to the Aleutian Islands," Royko said. "The first sergeant was shipped to Alaska. The base newspaper was shut down and I was made, in effect, a hotel clerk for the last two months of my enlistment. I had a newspaper shot out from under me. I didn't even know I had an exposé."

Still, he had found his calling. During his time on the base newspaper he signed on an assistant, a Chicagoan from Hyde Park named Stan Koven who was the same rank as Royko but had less time in the service. What Koven did have was a journalism degree—he'd also worked for Associated Press—and a question for his superior, Royko: "How did you ever convince them you'd worked on a newspaper?" The two clicked, however. Royko recalled, "Between his experience and expertise and my flair for the con job, we won awards." Koven got out of the service first and scouted the newspaper jobs. When Royko got out, on March 11, 1956, Koven told him about an opening on the *Lincoln-Belmont Booster,* a Chicago-area semiweekly owned by the Lerner chain.

"I talked to my wife about it," Royko recalled, "and she said why don't you give it a year or so, and if you don't like it, you can go in a different direction."

Royko (far right), looking skeptical. As
a young reporter he learned that little
of consequence comes out of a politician's press conference.

cisco wh
re town. So City Ha

t to a public minimum. If ol
w laws that did.

On the other hand, there w
omebody in City Hall saw a c
r two, Daley wasn't given to
ed to: Don't get caught.
But that's Chicago, too. Tl
you made it, but if you mad
demanded that dr
em rent

2
Glory Days at the *Daily News*

Royko took the job with the Lerner paper, but on March 12, 1956—the day after he left the air force—he also filled out an application for the City News Bureau of Chicago, a legendary agency that served the city's big dailies while providing training for young reporters.

In his City News application, under "biographical data," Royko wrote: "Though my formal education is limited, I have acquired substantial experience because of my good fortune in working with professional journalists. The O'Hare News was a weekly 8 page letterpress newspaper. Our staff was generally limited to two and we handled everything from the news gathering to the layout and distribution. I have no professional interests other than journalism and would be willing to start at the lowest position, financially and otherwise."

Under "special interests," Royko wrote: "My recreational interests consist of golf, boating, and reading."

After six months with the Lerner paper, Royko joined the City News, where he really began to learn his trade under a crusty, irascible, and brilliant editor named Arnold Dornfeld. As Royko later wrote, Dornfeld taught the following: "Accuracy. Speed. Determination. An eye for a story and an ear for a quote. The willingness to jump out of bed at any hour and rush out to a triple murder or a raging fire. He made you think it was a natural, normal way to live."

In the down hours, there were other lessons. Royko remembered: "There were Saturdays or Sundays at his old frame house on a few acres of farmland in a distant rural suburban area. He built the house himself, and it looked like it. . . . He'd gather the young reporters and their wives or girlfriends around his Franklin stove for a day of eating thick slices of ham, potato salad, dark rye bread, drinking good German beer, and listening to

Beethoven. Who else but Beethoven for a man who could roar as magnificently as the Fifth? If you sat through all nine symphonies, and appeared to appreciate them, he might invite you back for all the concerti. . . . And all the while you learned. About reporting, first, then about writing. About simplicity, brevity, clarity—but turning a phrase that gave a story that added touch of class."

It may be a cliché, but it's true—that was an education that he simply would not have received in journalism school. It was intense, fun, exhausting, and exhilarating. If it resembled something out of *The Front Page,* well, that play's coauthor, Charles MacArthur, once worked for City News. There was not much hand-wringing about the great issues of the day, and any exhibition of a social conscience would have been greeted with derision. But they got their stories. Sometimes they got them by posing as deputy coroners.

Royko explained: "If somebody did discover you were posing as a deputy coroner, in the pecking order of law enforcement, deputy coroner was so low, nobody was going to get indicted for posing as a deputy

coroner. You could get arrested for posing as a Chicago cop, or a state's attorney investigator—but a deputy coroner? If you were kind of scruffy-looking, people would believe you were a deputy coroner. We all posed as one thing or another. That's why no one hated the media in those days. We were all deputy coroners."

It did not mean making stuff up, though Royko saw some of that, too. Covering the murder of Chicago gangster Roger Touhy for City News, Royko interviewed people in all the buildings near the murder site. He went through the basements of the buildings. The next day, a Hearst

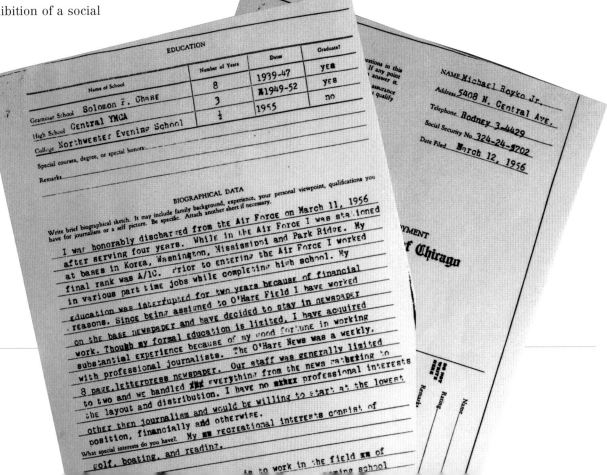

Royko's application to work for the City News Bureau.

paper blared an exclusive—We Know Where the Assassins Were Hiding!—and ran a picture of a basement room littered with cigarette butts. Royko had been there the day before—no cigarette butts. Maybe the Hearst photographer was a heavy smoker.

Royko made his own—legitimate—mark as a crime reporter covering the grisly deaths of two teenage girls, Patricia and Barbara Grimes, who were found frozen and naked in a ditch near suburban Willow Springs in January of 1957.

The following month, Royko interviewed at the *Chicago Daily News* with the paper's acting city editor, Maurice "Ritz" Fischer. The interview was going pretty well when Royko, acutely aware of the *Daily News*'s tradition as a "writer's paper" that featured major talents like Peter Lisagor and Ed Lahey, suddenly called a halt. "Mr. Fischer, I don't think there's any point in continuing this interview. I just don't have enough experience."

He went back to City News, developed his skills, and a year later knocked on the door of the *Daily News* again. A new city editor said the paper had no openings, nor did the other Chicago dailies—the *Tribune, Sun-Times,* and *American*. "First thing everybody said was, 'Why didn't you finish college?' " recalled Royko, who had attended some evening classes at Northwestern University. "That wasn't easy. It stays with you."

Royko at the *Daily News*: Tough, baloney-proof, headed for fame.

The pay was not among the attractions at City News, and by the fall of 1958, Carol was pregnant with their first child. Royko, now in his midtwenties, went so far as to audition for a TV job—combination news director, anchor, reporter—at a station in Fort Wayne, Indiana, but he was turned down for a failure to project. For a time Royko sold tombstones for Carol's parents, Fred and Mildred Duckman, who owned a funeral home on Central Avenue in Chicago. "He sold monuments and he was pretty good at it," said his brother, Bob.

But it wasn't what he wanted. In 1959, when he heard that the *Chicago Daily News* now had an opening, he applied and was sent to a place on Michigan Avenue to take a variety of tests. After two days, the paper's executive editor, Basil "Stuffy" Waters, called him in. "Those tests show that you are extremely intelligent and honest and you have a great natural ability for this business."

Said Royko, "I think those are great tests."

It was the start of a glorious, two-decade run at the *Chicago Daily News*. Of the paper, he said later: "It emphasized bright writing. Keep the stories short. It was the first paper in America to have a full time foreign service. It had more Pulitzer Prize winners than all the other Chicago papers combined. In its day it was a helluva paper." Carol was working for a doctor in the Logan Square area. They often met at a Greek restaurant after work, where they'd sit and talk about the future.

Royko loved the paper and the people who worked on it, and he even put up with an early editor on the four-to-midnight shift who took a dislike to him and tried everything to get Royko to quit. "Forget it," he told the editor eventually. "This is the job I want and I'm going to put up with anything you can dish out."

Royko outlasted him, and that clash was a departure, because for the most part, the men—and the *Daily News* staff did consist mostly of men—were Royko's brethren.

"When I broke into newspapers," Royko said, "most of my mentors—the senior reporters and editors—were part of the Depression, World War II generation. They didn't take themselves quite as seriously. They liked being newspapermen. You never heard the word 'career.' Everyone had worked in one kind of grungy job or another. At the *Daily News,* one of the rewrite men had been a prisoner of war. Another guy limped because he had taken a Japanese bullet in his heel. Our music critic, a very quiet, sensitive man—his wife once showed me a picture of him sitting in his fighter plane. He was a World War II ace. These guys had a different attitude about life. They were more forgiving. If we nailed a politician, nobody wanted him to go to jail. We nailed him. We got a story. Throw him back. It's like a fish. We'll catch him again later."

Royko recalled that the *Daily News* man who had been a POW—at Stalag 17—was known to get overserved occasionally at lunch. "He'd go out to lunch on Thursday and you wouldn't see him again until maybe Monday. He was on a toot. You don't have people doing that today. Newspapers won't tolerate it. If a guy went out and didn't come back you'd figure he got lost jogging. You don't have newspaper guys going out for a beer after work. They're serious. They jog. They go out during lunch and swim fifty laps."

Part of that change, surely, is to the good. A lifestyle that does not include a collapsed liver by age forty-five is probably a good thing. And who could argue about equal opportunity for women and people of color? The few women in the *Daily News* newsroom when Royko started included Georgie Anne Geyer, later a renowned foreign correspondent and columnist, and Lois Wille, who became an editorial page editor and Pulitzer Prize winner. But that was later. "Both of them went on to great careers," Royko said. "But at the time they got assignments like, 'Our gal here.' Lois Wille is the single best newspaper person I have ever known, but they sent her out to do screwball stuff—brush a rhinoceros' tooth or something."

But those hard-living, blue-collar white males brought a few things to the job—not least, the street smarts of a corner bookie or beat cop—that are sorely missed. No politician or other stuffed-shirt could con them. They knew their city inside out. In his early days Royko and his reporter buddies used to sit in a bar and play a game called street corners. Somebody would throw out an intersection, and if you couldn't name at least one business on a corner of it, you were in disgrace.

Royko's friend Jimmy Breslin, today in his late sixties and writing two columns a week for *Newsday,* spoke to all this in his 1996 memoir, *I Want to Thank My Brain for Remembering Me*.

"The way I had it is all gone now," Breslin wrote. "The bars are gone, the drinkers gone. There remain the smartest, healthiest newspeople in the history of the business. And they are so boring that they kill the business right in front of you. A central reason why newspaper circulation is dropping so alarmingly is that reporters have all the excitement of a Formica table."

Breslin continued, "Newspaper managements love the new fashion of news reporters, however, because they cause no trouble. They go to some exercise place at lunch and after work they go right home to dinner. It is so much better for marriages, and calmness at work. Their children might be the first generation in a news family to have a somewhat normal life. And since words from a newspaper come from nervous energy and not propriety, the readers get robbed and the news reporters never live."

Nor is Breslin enamored of the computerized newsroom. "The computers took the verve out of the whole newsroom and the charm out of the stories. The words on the reporter's screen now were so neat that there could be nothing wrong. . . . The copy happened to be as boring as it was neat. The reporters all have at least one degree from a good college and can speak at least one other language, but they have been brought up on television and they stare at the computer terminal with the passivity of someone watching a situation comedy. The verbs become so passive that the sentences seem to stop for a commercial."

While later in life Royko loved exploring the Internet, at the same time he installed a computer program that duplicated the clatter of a typewriter, "the same sound that an old-time typewriter makes," he said. "Once in a while I turn it on. I like it—I like hearing the rattle. It's really fun. You can even buy fonts that you can install, that instead of getting this nice clean copy, you get this old-time typewriter font, with broken keys and cracked letters."

When he started at the *Daily News,* he didn't have to pretend. The newsroom was noisy, bustling, full of inspired lunacy. Enraged editors chased each other around desks brandishing copy spikes, and a horse-racing writer once sprawled naked on a desk so a masseur who had hit big on his recommendation could administer a massage. Royko's contribution was to occasionally climb on top of a desk and offer his version of a love affair between Eleanor Roosevelt and Adlai Stevenson.

Mostly, though, he worked. Switched to days, Royko was put on the county government beat. All the beat reporters were asked to do a weekly column. Most pulled together chatty little items that hadn't been strong enough to make the paper during the week. Royko's was different from the start. He profiled eccentric characters who hung around the county building, he detailed bureaucratic idiocies, he told a story in a few hundred words that were much more alive and entertaining than anything else in the paper.

"I don't think people really noticed it," Royko said. "But it was well received by the people at the paper. And I said if I can make this crap interesting from the county government, county politics, I can go beyond that."

In early 1963 he told an editor he respected at the *Daily News,* Larry Fanning, that he felt ready for a change. Other papers were offering better money, and Seymour Simon, a political heavyweight in Chicago, had asked Royko to handle his public relations. Fanning asked what he wanted. Royko said he wanted a stab at a local column.

"I didn't like being under the control of editors. Being told: 'This is what we want you to cover and this is how we want you to handle it,' " Royko said. "Not that I was being told to do things I felt were wrong; I just didn't want them shaping the story for me. I didn't like being assigned to dull stories."

Another difference between Royko and many young, ambitious journalists today is that, while he was ambitious enough to covet a column, Royko had little interest, at first, in commenting on national affairs. Today, as soon as a columnist locates the Send button on his computer he's weighing in on the White House, the space program, or some world economic crisis. Next thing you know, some farm team McLaughlin Group wants him on their panel show and with that, can stardom be far behind?

Hard as it is to believe, on first getting his column in the *Daily News* Royko actually turned down the paper's request that he cover the 1964 national political conventions. He told the editors: "I write about local stuff. I want the readers to get to know me. The way they get to know me is by my writing about something that I know about and they know about."

He got his wish. "I started it with the understanding it would be a Chicago column. That was it. They wanted a Chicago column, a Chicago voice, and I'd covered politics and city and county government, I'd lived here all my life, I was probably as equipped as anybody my age at the paper to do a column at that time."

On September 6, 1963, two weeks before his thirty-first birthday, Royko wrote his first "Chicago" column for the *Daily News*. He told the story of a Chicago cab driver whose tavern had been demolished in the name of urban renewal. The column appeared in the back of the paper, on the "columnists' page" near the editorials, and for a few months he did only two or three a week. But by January of 1964, after the paper's lead columnist, Jack Mabley, resigned to join the *Chicago American,* Royko was writing five a week. They remained deep inside for a couple of years until the *Daily News* conducted an eye-opening study to learn what was popular in the paper.

"They did a readership survey and found I had more readers on page 14 than the front page stories had, so they moved me to page 3," Royko said. He actually fought the switch. "I didn't want to be on page 3 of the *Daily News*. It was a hard news page and I didn't think I could write columns I thought would be fun on a real hard news page. I was quite happy back on the column page. [Moving up] was really stressful for a while. I thought every day I have to come up with something really important, and that isn't my style. I like to write about things that aren't important once in a while."

They did a readership survey and found I had more readers on page 14 than the front page stories had, so they moved me to page 3. I didn't want to be on page 3 of the *Daily News*. It was a hard news page and I didn't think I could write columns I thought would be fun on a real hard news page. I was quite happy back on the column page. [Moving up] was really stressful for a while.

One subject of great importance that Royko did visit—actually traveled for—was civil rights. Many years later Royko was asked which of all his columns he considered memorable. It was not a question he liked answering. But he said, "I suppose in '65, the stuff in Selma and Montgomery, the freedom march, I was pretty proud of those." Royko described the various atrocities committed in Alabama out of racial hatred. It made many of the *Daily News* readers uncomfortable, probably more so because the theme underlining the columns was, Don't be smug, Chicago.

"I knew Chicago," Royko said. "I knew attitudes up here, and sure enough, [Dr. Martin Luther] King didn't get hit by a brick in the south. He got one off his head up here."

If some readers were put off by those early columns on the ugliness of institutionalized racism, what must they have thought when Royko poked fun—no, ridiculed—Chicago politicians, the esteemed Mayor Richard J. Daley foremost among them? Well, a lot of readers loathed it, but many loved it—and everybody read it. Perhaps it took a while to articulate, but on a gut level people seemed to realize no one had ever written about politics—in this most political of towns—in the way Royko was doing it.

"When I started my column," Royko said, "I got up every morning thinking: Who's going to do what? What crazy thing is going to happen today? . . . There was so much goofy stuff going on. You had the Machine. That was it. You had the Machine. If you couldn't get columns out of the old Daley Machine—anybody could have done it. I'd go to City Council meetings and just sit there and describe what actually happened."

Imagine that—describing events as they actually happened and quoting people as they actually spoke. "That was one reason I wanted a column," Royko said. "I found that Chicago politics as it was being covered didn't really reflect reality. The beat reporters would clean up the language. They would make really idiotic people sound reasonably normal. And I wanted to write about them the way they really were. . . . There was no shortage of investigative reporting. Trying to nail the bad guys. But there was something I thought was lacking: the color of it. The humor. The comic scene. That's the way I felt about pols. They were comedic material."

Not surprisingly, the pols were not amused. Daley went so far as to have a public relations assistant—the mayor would never admit to even knowing who Royko was—tell the city press corps that if Royko kept attending press conferences, Daley would quit having them. The columnist quit going. Nobody says anything worth reporting at a press conference anyway.

It was going to be all the harder for Daley—or anyone

else—to ignore Royko's presence in Chicago after the July 1, 1966, issue of *Time* magazine hit the streets. It contained a glowing profile of Royko.

Under the headline "Love & Hate in Chicago," *Time* noted: "In a city where newspaper columnists are almost always civic boosters, Mike Royko, 33, is a constant critic. A foe of all forms of cant and pomp, he carries on a love-hate affair with his home town. He writes tenderly of its ethnic neighborhoods, its traditions and folkways; he fires at will at its politicians and their pretensions."

Time was particularly impressed with a column Royko wrote pummeling Chicago Fire Commissioner Robert Quinn. " 'Remember,' " the magazine quoted Royko, " 'back in 1959 Quinn was the person who put Chicago under its first atomic alert. He blew all the air-raid sirens late one night because he got a kick out of the White Sox clinching a pennant. And anyone who can talk his way out of sending people into the streets in their shorts to await doomsday can talk his way out of anything.' "

Later, someone asked Royko how Quinn felt about him. "Quinn hates my guts, and I can't blame him. If anybody wrote about me like I write about Quinn, I'd hate his guts too."

By the time the profile in *Time* appeared, Chicagoans bumping into each other on the street, in the elevator, or at the office water cooler had begun to utter a peculiar phrase: "Ju-read-Royko?" You had better have, because everyone else had.

A number of things stood out about the column. For starters, Royko's durability. That he could do five columns a week of consistent quality—and at one time he went up to six a week to help boost circulation at the *Daily News*—over weeks and months and eventually years was looked upon with awe by colleagues and readers alike. Another thing was his range. In a given week he could do an investigative piece on corruption in the Daley machine, a tender-funny neighborhood fable featuring Slats Grobnik, a pained and insightful sports bit on why the Cubs were blowing it again, a hilarious social commentary on jogging, and, to finish it off, an outraged tale of a little guy with no

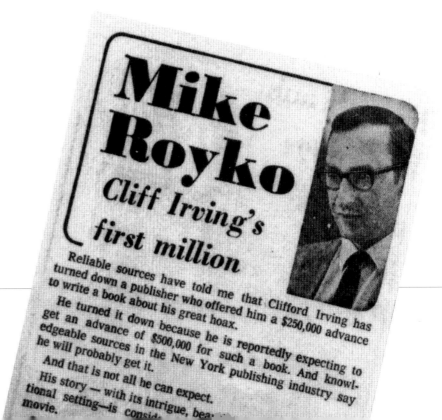

Mike Royko

Cliff Irving's first million

Reliable sources have told me that Clifford Irving has turned down a publisher who offered him a $250,000 advance to write a book about his great hoax.

He turned it down because he is reportedly expecting to get an advance of $500,000 for such a book. And knowledgeable sources in the New York publishing industry say he will probably get it.

And that is not all he can expect.

His story — with its intrigue, bea... tional setting—is consid... movie.

clout getting pushed around by authority. Five days, five columns, five subjects, five home runs.

No wonder Tim Weigel, a Chicago sportscaster and good friend of Royko's, once said of spending time with the columnist, "You felt like you were hanging out with Mozart."

When that kind of praise started flowing, Royko dodged it. He'd often say that his friends Nelson Algren and Studs Terkel were small giants—Algren the gritty novelist, Terkel the oral historian—while he was a tall midget. Bob Greene, a Chicago columnist who spent much of his career being compared to Royko, though their columns were vastly different in tone and purpose, had a conversation with him in the late sixties during which Greene, somewhat awed, kept insisting Royko was the best columnist in the world. Finally Royko said, "That's like being the elephant who's best at sticking its thumb up its trunk."

But young reporters looked up to Royko—they couldn't help it. On New Year's Day 1967, Royko was—where else?—at his desk at the *Daily News*. It was snowing hard in Chicago, and by evening few people were in the building. One was a fresh-faced, part-time *Sun-Times* staffer—the two papers shared quarters—named Roger Ebert, later to become famous as a movie critic. He bumped into Royko at the coffee machine.

Nodding out at the snow, Royko said, "How you getting home?"

"I don't know."

"I'll give you a lift," Royko said.

"He was in his thirties, but looked older," Ebert recalled later. "He was one of those guys like Robert Mitchum who always looked about fifty, no matter what age he was."

Driving through the snow, Royko stopped at a drug store at North and Milwaukee, explaining he had to pick up a prescription. Waiting for it to be filled, they had a drink at the little stand-up bar under the El (elevated train) tracks. "Guys stop off here for a quick shot on their way to work in the morning," Royko said. Ebert was pinching himself. He could scarcely believe he was hanging out with Mike Royko. They could hear the Chicago Blackhawks hockey game on a radio behind the bar. "What a game!" Ebert said. "The Blackhawks seem to be scoring every thirty seconds!"

"You jerk," Royko said. "That's the highlights."

Later that year, Royko came up with the first of what would be several contests for his readers, the best known being Royko's Ribfest in the early 1980s. In 1967, shortly after the conclusion of the oh-so-tony Westminster Dog Show at Madison Square Garden, Royko announced he would be hosting the First Annual Mixed Breed (Mongrel)

Dog Show. His column described some of the categories of judging, including an award for the dog that answered the fewest number of commands and a particular favorite: The Dog That Barks the Longest for No Known Reason.

He held the event at Soldier Field near Burnham Harbor. In a sense, it was a success. It was a sunny afternoon, and the hundreds of entrants included some of the dumbest and mangiest beasts in the Midwest. Van Gordon Sauter, later to be president of CBS News but then covering the contest for the *Daily News,* wrote that one of the winning dogs resembled a foot scraper.

Royko, though, as good a student of human nature as he was, hadn't thought this one through. People were taking it seriously! They really wanted their dogs to win! Royko ran into a journalist friend and shook his head. "They don't see anything funny about it. This is the worst thing I've ever experienced."

Another 1967 event was more satisfying. Further confirming Royko's status, the Henry Regnery Company of Chicago brought out a collection of his *Daily News* columns under the title *Up Against It*. Royko dedicated it to Larry Fanning, the editor who had given him the shot at a column; Bill Mauldin, the famed World War II and political cartoonist, wrote an introduction.

"Royko is like his city," Mauldin wrote. "He has sharp elbows, he thinks sulphur and soot are natural ingredients of the atmosphere, and he has an astonishing capacity for idealism and love devoid of goo. He has written about Chicago in a way that has never been matched. It will probably never be matched in the future, either, because by purchasing this book you have contributed to the enrichment and corruption of this fine boy. But that's his problem."

If Royko had a true problem, it was finding time and balancing the various aspects of what was becoming a hectic life with many persistent demands. A 1979 *Esquire* magazine profile of Royko by William Brashler noted that by the mid-to-late 1960s, "his wife, according to close friends, became a widow to the column."

It wasn't just Carol, because she and Mike now had two sons, David, born in 1959, and Rob, born four years later. Until 1969, when they moved to a home in the Edgebrook neighborhood, they lived on North Central Avenue on the second and third floors of Carol's parents' funeral home. Rob Royko says that one of his first memories as a kid was being told not to go downstairs. "Everyone said, 'Never go

Mike and Carol in a light-hearted moment.

To show how powerful he was, I wound up being [Daley's] number one adversary, for a good many years. I was his number one adversary. I'd like to be in that position. Running a city and some meatball on a newspaper is the only guy I have to worry about. He didn't have to worry about who ran against him. Why do you want to climb Mt. Everest? Because it's there. He was there.

downstairs. Never go downstairs.' So of course I finally went downstairs and there was a stiff."

But except for their dad's absence, it wasn't a bad place to grow up. Carol's parents were by all accounts wonderful people, kind and gentle. "A Norman Rockwell family," David Royko says. Of course, Rockwell's families usually didn't have strangers throwing eggs at the side of the house or bricks through windows. David's very first recollection of growing up—probably about 1965—is of walking home from school and finding a group of picketers standing outside. "At first I was a little bit scared, because I didn't know if I'd be able to get into my house," he recalls. Carol came out and brought him in, and David said, "What are they doing out there?" He knew his dad worked for the newspaper, but he was too young to understand the job. His dad went to work like other dads. David went to look out the window and—*splat!*—an egg from a picketer hit the side of the house. And what was the source of their rage?

"It had to do with a column my dad wrote on integration," David says. "It was pro-integration, it might have been busing, I'm not sure. But it was a liberal stand, which was nothing unusual for him, and it angered people."

Another time, in the middle of the night, a brick came through a window, barely missing Rob, who lay sleeping in bed. "I think my dad went down to the bar, found the guy who threw it, and confronted him," Rob says.

It was curious to have such things happening at the same time a magazine like *Time* had published a glowing profile of him. Royko was quickly becoming famous, but as his family learned, it was a unique kind of celebrity. "My mom got the best and the roughest stuff," David says. "The job, the column, it was all so wonderful for this stuff to be happening to Dad. But the downside was that it was an incredibly stressful time."

David continues, "That was hard on my mother. All of a sudden there were fans, everybody wants to buy you a drink, everybody wants to get into a fight with you, everybody wants, you know, your attention of some kind. And he was so provocative. I mean, it's one thing to want a moment with your average celebrity, but everybody had an emotional reaction to him, one way or another."

Royko, at the paper eight, ten, twelve hours a day, escaped the stress on softball fields—he captained the *Daily News*'s sixteen-inch softball team for years, often playing fifty or more games a summer—and in bars. His family, meanwhile, was at home. Occasionally Carol would show up after a game to play the juke box and hear stories of that night's heroics on the diamond. But mostly she was with the kids, waiting. "We never had a family dinner," says David Royko, who now works as a family psychologist for Cook County. "My mother tried very hard to get family stuff going. One time she had me make a list, the things I'd like to do with Dad."

Rob Royko, who owns a music store in suburban McHenry, remembers seeing his dad on Sundays. (The dedication to *Boss,* the biography of Richard J. Daley that Royko wrote while doing five columns a week, reads "For Dave and Rob and all the Sundays missed.") Rob recalls, "Maybe he wasn't around as much as most dads. But I'd rather have had him for a dad and have him home less than most dads who are around all the time."

It is altogether fitting that in March of 1964, just a few months after Royko began his *Daily News* column, an unusual bar opened in a converted garage in the darkness of lower Hubbard Street. From the door of the Billy Goat Tavern you could throw a shot glass and hit a woman shopping for a $3,500 dress on Michigan Avenue. Go inside, however, and you might be back on Armitage Avenue. Tap beer, wobbly bar stools, wisecracks—Royko was home.

The Billy Goat was the creation of William Sianis, who had owned a place of the same name on Madison Street but made the move in 1964 at the suggestion of a friend who worked on the *Chicago Tribune.* The *Trib,* the *Sun-Times, Daily News,* and *American* were all within crawling distance of the new location, so how could it miss? Sianis always owned a goat, and legend had it he had tried to take the animal to Wrigley Field to see the Cubs play a World Series game in 1945. When the goat was refused entrance, Sianis put a hex on the Cubs, and of course they haven't won a pennant since.

Sianis's nephew, Sam Sianis, born in Greece in 1935, took over the Billy Goat after his uncle's death and became one of Royko's closest friends. Sam's fractured English and the crazy things that happen in any tavern made for great columns, but on a deeper level Royko admired how hard Sam worked to make the bar a success. He swept the floor, worked the grill, tossed the drunks, and made friends with the reporters and pressmen who were his regular customers. "In those days the news people were a lot of fun," Sianis said. "We had a lot of laughs." His first impression of Royko? "He was a real guy. He wasn't a phony. He wrote what he lived and what he saw. He was like my brother."

Billy Goat proprietor Sam Sianis said of Royko: "He was like my brother."

The Billy Goat Tavern, made
famous in Royko's columns and
the "cheezborger" sketches on
Saturday Night Live.

Royko made the Billy Goat famous in his columns, and Sianis in turn would take care of him over the years. Royko drank a lot and had a complicated relationship with alcohol. Clearly it damaged him physically, and the fact that he would at times drink himself into near oblivion suggests dark personal vistas. But there were other times, many other times, after softball, after finishing a difficult column, when relaxing in a tavern was just about the happiest thing in the world for Mike Royko. He grew up in bars, and as an adult he chose bar people for friends. When he spoke of it, which wasn't often, Royko said that having a few drinks helped him unwind from the pressure of the high-wire act he performed five times a week for an audience in the millions.

Royko once wrote an introduction for a book on Chicago bars and nightlife that was authored by Rick Kogan, a Chicago journalist of later vintage than the columnist who nevertheless became his close friend. Kogan, too, is acquainted with the highs and lows of booze and says of Royko, "Drinking was a way for him to sort of soften the edges of what was, like it or not or understand it or not, a very, very demanding task. Mike writing a column was like a surgeon going in. Only the surgeon not knowing exactly what kind of surgery he has to perform. What an incredibly daunting task."

No doubt all eyes were on Royko when the Democrats brought their national convention to Chicago in the summer of 1968. He welcomed the Dems with a scathing column on the biggest Democrat of them all in Chicago, Mayor Richard J. Daley.

"To assist visitors," Royko wrote, "I have prepared a primer on the mayor. . . . Daley likes to build things. He likes high-rises, expressways, parking garages, municipal buildings and anything else that requires a ribbon-cutting ceremony and can be financed through federal funds. He isn't that enthusiastic about small things, such as people. Daley does not like civil rights demonstrators, rebellious community organizations, critics of the mediocre school

Demonstrators and National
Guard troops confront one another
at the 1968 Democratic National
Convention in Chicago.

system, critics of any kind or people who argue with him." And with the convention due in, whom would Daley support for the Democratic nomination?

"The mayor," Royko wrote, "will consider which candidate is the wisest, the noblest, the most inspiring, the best qualified. Then he will pick the one with the best chance of winning. In his parades, the politicians march up front. No matter how pretty they play, the flute players walk behind the horses."

The convention itself, in late August of 1968, was a debacle. Earlier in the year Daley had been rocked to his core when the city's West Side erupted into violence and vandalism after the murder of Martin Luther King Jr. Now anti–Vietnam War demonstrators with flowers in their hair were streaming into the city, pitching tents, and threatening to make Chicago look ridiculous on national television. Daley called in the FBI and called out the National Guard and had his own police force so on edge that if someone had popped a balloon at headquarters he'd have been cuffed and beaten by half a dozen officers.

Ironically, Daley was privately against the war. But all his life in politics told him that if you were pushed, you pushed back. In the convention hall, supporters of peace candidates George McGovern and Gene McCarthy shouted Daley down when he took the rostrum. His face red and his eyes wild, he hollered back. And he sent his cops into

the street outside the Hilton Hotel and into Lincoln Park on the near North Side where they pummeled just about anybody who got in their way. Royko's colleague John Linstead, a *Daily News* reporter, had his head split open and was left lying in the street. Royko's cold and angry columns about the convention earned him one of journalism's highest awards, the Heywood Broun, presented by the American Newspaper Guild.

They were read all over the country. Royko wasn't yet syndicated, but the *Daily News* offered a package of columns and features for sale to other papers around the United States, and Royko was the top attraction. Another collection—*I May Be Wrong, But I Doubt It*—was brought out by Regnery. Most significant, there was a louder, more daunting, literary drum beating. The convention had made national figures of two Chicagoans—Daley and his fiercest and most astute critic, Royko.

"Somebody had to do it," Royko said later, pointing out that the newspaper editorial pages, and even most Republicans, liked Daley and indulged his flaws. "To show how powerful he was, I wound up as his number one adversary, for a good many years. I was his number one adversary. I'd like to be in that position. Running a city and some meatball on a newspaper is the only guy I have to worry about. He didn't have to worry about who ran against him. Why do you want

to climb Mt. Everest? Because it's there. He was there."

The mountain got a little higher when a number of Royko's close friends in Chicago—along with East Coast agents and editors—began urging him to do a book on Daley. Royko later credited Studs Terkel "for talking me into it," and other Chicagoans—politicos, iconoclasts, writers, and journalists—also were encouraging him, Saul Alinsky and Nelson Algren among them. Alinsky was an impassioned and embattled civil rights leader and community organizer, and Algren, well, if Royko had ever articulated it, he might have said Algren was his literary hero.

The columnist later said he'd first heard the name in a tent in Korea. A guy in a nearby bunk tossed a paperback at him and said, "Here's a book about Chicago. You want it?" The book was *The Man with the Golden Arm,* and it had won the first-ever National Book Award for fiction. The cover copy said it was set in a Chicago slum around Division Street. Royko was offended. "Slum?" he thought. "That's no slum. That's my neighborhood."

The book itself knocked him out. "Here was somebody named Nelson Algren writing about Division Street and Milwaukee Avenue, and the dope heads and boozers and the card hustlers. The kind of broken people Algren liked to describe as responding to the city's brawny slogan 'I Will' with a painful: 'But What If I Can't?' "

Royko met Algren shortly after beginning his *Daily News* column. The author had a party in his small flat—like most of his characters, Algren was always a little short of cash—in the old Damen–North–Milwaukee Avenue area, overlooking Wicker Park. At that gathering Royko mentioned to Algren that his favorite of Algren's books was *The Neon Wilderness,* a collection of short stories set in Chicago, where Algren lived from 1911 to 1974. "I was afraid he might be offended," Royko recalled, "since he considered himself foremost a novelist. But he listened, nodded politely, and said, 'That's interesting.' "

A friendship developed, close enough that, when a new edition of *The Neon Wilderness* was published in 1967, Algren dedicated it to Royko, a gesture the deeply touched columnist called "one of the nicest things anyone ever did for me."

In May of 1981, David Royko came to visit his father at his home and walked in to find him crying. "He was just sobbing and I was concerned. This was something you never saw. I asked him what was wrong and he didn't really answer." David went to another room and in a few minutes Mike stood in the doorway. He apologized for not answering, but he had just learned that Nelson Algren had died.

Royko wrote a beautiful eulogy and then in another column suggested to the "stiffs on the city council" that it might be a nice gesture to name a small street near Wicker Park after this giant of American literature. To Royko's surprise, Mayor Jane Byrne took him up on it and a street sign was prepared. But then, as Royko later recounted, the neighborhood's alderman began to get phone calls from constituents who didn't want the hassle of changing documents to reflect their new address. The council backed out—no Algren Street. Royko could only shake his head. At least Nelson would likely have laughed at the ironic ending, almost as if it was from one of his stories.

Algren was among those Royko thanked on the acknowledgments page of *Boss*. But it was the dedication—to his boys "and all the Sundays missed"—that told of the awesome task of writing a daily column, for Royko did not take a leave of absence from the paper while researching, writing, and then promoting the book. "After three years I was about ten years older," Royko said.

His son David remembers waking on a Sunday morning while his dad was researching the book and seeing him dressed for church. "It was weird to see him in a suit," David says. "I said to my mom, 'Where's Dad going?' She said, 'Ask him.' " David did, and his dad grinned: "To spy on Daley."

Top **Nelson Algren (left) and Royko at a book signing for Royko's first collection of columns.**

Bottom **Algren was the Chicago writer Royko most admired. Both loved the city but felt compelled to criticize it.**

It was a point of pride that the columns not suffer while the book was being written. "If anything, I worked harder on the columns because I was very worried I might let the column slip, the book would distract me," said Royko.

He typed the last page of *Boss* late on a Saturday afternoon in 1970 in his office at the *Daily News*. Royko ended his book by quoting something Alderman Paddy Bauler had said in 1955, when Daley was first elected: "Chicago ain't ready for reform yet." Royko's conclusion: "And in 1970, like it or not, it wasn't getting any."

Royko pulled the page from the typewriter, put it under the others in the large stack, and walked to Riccardo's, a restaurant and bar on Rush Street near the newspapers. The bar was quiet and Royko ordered a martini, not his usual drink of choice. This was, after all, quite a moment.

The bartender, who knew him, said, "What's going on, Mike? Celebrating?"

"I guess so," Royko said. "I just finished a book."

"Yeah?" the bartender said. "Me, too." He reached under the bar and handed Royko a paperback. "You can read it. It's by Mickey Spillane."

There was a little more excitement after the book's publication. It sold 125,000 copies in hardcover and more than a million in paperback. Billy Goat Tavern owner Sam Sianis recalls Royko coming into the bar around that time and saying, "Sam, come over here. I want to show you something." It was a check for $7,000—the first royalties. "This is the first time in my life I've seen a check like this."

If anything, its critical success was even larger. "It is the best book ever written about a city of this country," Jimmy Breslin wrote. "And perhaps it will stand as the best book ever written about the American condition at this time. It comes at you from the saloons and neighborhoods, the police stations and political back rooms. It is about lies and viciousness, about the worship of cement and the hatred toward blacks, about a troubling cowardice that hides behind religion and patriotism while the poor get clubbed and killed. It is written with a deep understanding of the evil and terrible power of mediocrity."

"Excellent. First rate," wrote Nicholas von Hoffman. "The best thing ever written about Mayor Daley and fully worthy of Mike Royko, the best newspaper writer in the country."

There were dissenters. The *Chicago Tribune* opined that *Boss* made Daley into a one-dimensional villain. They were shouted down, though, by admirers like Russell Baker: "Royko is the best thing to come out of Chicago journalism since Ben Hecht. He has wit, style, high intelligence. . . . The book? It's Daley; Royko's got him to the life. And it's Chicago. Even if you've never been there you know it's Chicago."

In January of 1971 Royko's brother, Bob, had married a woman from Madison, Wisconsin, named Geri Caravello. Mike served as their best man, and when the young couple went to Aspen for a honeymoon, he had the pleasure of being able to send them an early copy of *Boss,* along with a note: "Hey, Kid: This is a genuine first edition. I figure all of them will be first editions. So you get the first of the first. I ask one favor of you: Do not let anyone else read this. It won't be published until the middle of March and I don't want anybody reading it free. Let them buy, buy, buy, so I will be rich, rich, rich. I'm also enclosing a copy of Breslin's book [*The Gang That Couldn't Shoot Straight*]. It's about Sicilians. His wife is a Sicilian [as was Bob's]. I read it and it makes my blood run cold. I caution you, Bobby, to frisk her before retiring at night. Those people use Stilettos." He signed it "Love, Mick"—the family always called him by his childhood nickname.

He may have been being modest, but he was certainly wrong about the number of printings of *Boss.* There was even a Japanese edition—eventually Royko had a student fan club in that country. Royko took a copy of the Japanese edition home—the family by then was living in a house in Edgebrook, on the city's far Northwest Side— handed it to his son Rob, and said, "I'll give you a hun-

dred dollars if you can read one word in this book." Rob flipped through and came to the title page: Boss. "I argued with him. My mom argued with him. He ended up buying me a hundred dollars worth of stuff."

In 1972 Royko was awarded the Pulitzer Prize for commentary. It was the ultimate testimony to Royko's determination not to let his column slip while he worked on the Daley book. How did Royko learn he had won journalism's highest award? He was in Wisconsin visiting his brother when he got a message to call his secretary at the *Daily News.* Before making the call, he used the bathroom.

"So I'm standing there with my schwanz in my hand," he recalled later. Why was the paper tracking him down? "And then it came to me. 'Oh, wait a minute. Holy Christ, I won the Pulitzer.' It was not the way I would have wanted it to be. The way to win the Pulitzer is you want to be in the office when it comes in over the wires and everybody cheers. But this is how I found out—by reading the toilet bowl."

By the time of *Boss* and the Pulitzer, Royko had people he referred to as his "Dr. Watsons, Igors, Tontos and most valued friends." Four years into the *Daily News* column, Royko got a full-time assistant to help chase down leads, answer the phone, and try to instill a little order into his chaotic universe. The sixteen journalists who held the position over the years described it as a thrilling, unnerv-

ing, priceless opportunity to work alongside a master.
"I was in a constant state of uncertainty when I worked
for him," said Ellen Warren, today a *Tribune* columnist, in
1979. "But those fourteen months were the most important thing I've done so far in my career. That and covering the civil war in Lebanon."

Royko referred to his assistants as legmen—leg creatures, with the advent of political correctness, a concept
Royko did not embrace. They in turn called him Mr. Big
or simply Big. In 1982, when Royko published a collection
of his columns titled *Sez Who? Sez Me,* he not only dedicated it to his assistants, he had a party at his home and
gave them each a personally inscribed copy. In each, he
had written: "You were my best. Don't tell the others."

Royko loved practical jokes. Hanke (pronounced Hanky)
Gratteau, who worked as his assistant at three different
newspapers and today is the *Tribune*'s city editor, says
Royko could sense mornings when perhaps your brain was
not doing its best work—"since you'd been out with him the
night before"—and he would pounce. Maybe it was the
piece of foam that looked like granite that he'd hurl your
way or the stunningly realistic fishing lure that appeared
out of nowhere. "He'd sneak up behind me and drop this
wiggling worm in my face just to get me to scream."

Occasionally, Gratteau was a co-conspirator. One day
when they were with the *Sun-Times,* Royko spotted

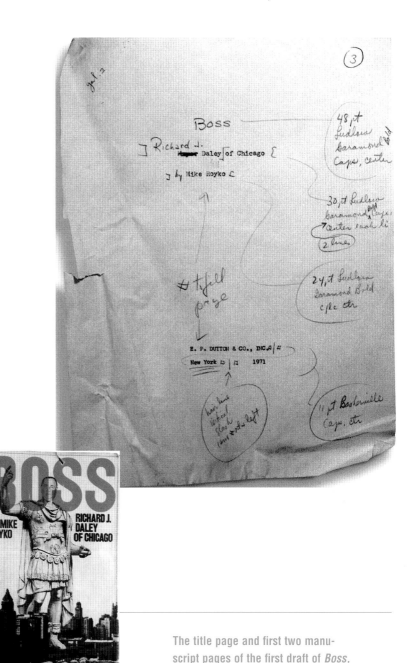

The title page and first two manu-
script pages of the first draft of *Boss*,
Royko's classic biography of Richard
J. Daley and his political machine.

Chapter I

William Kunstler: What is your name?

Witness: Richard Joseph Daley.

William Kunstler: What is your occupation?

Witness: I am the mayor of the city of Chicago.

The work day begins early. Sometime after seven o'clock a black limousine glides out of the garage of the police station on the corner, moves less than a block, and stops in front of a pink bungalow at 3536 S. Lowe Avenue. Policeman Alphonsus Gilhooly, walking in front of the house, nods to the detective at the wheel of the limousine.

It's an unlikely house for such a car. A passing stranger might think that a rich man had come back to visit his people in their old neighborhood. It's the kind of sturdy brick house, common to Chicago, that a fireman or printer would buy. Thousands like it were put up by contractors in the 1920's and 1930's from standard blueprints in an architectural style fondly dubbed "carpenter's delight."

The outside of that pink house is deceiving. A stranger going inside would find it furnished in expensive, colonial-style furniture, the basement panelled in fine wood, and two days a week a woman comes in to help with the cleaning.

MORE

The blue-blood bankers from downtown aren't invited, although they would like to be, and neither are men who have been governors, senators, and ambassadors. The people who come in the evening or on Sunday are old friends from the neighborhood, the relatives, people who take their coats off when they walk in the door, and loosen their ties.

Danaher is one of them, and his relationship is so close that he has served as an emotional whipping boy, so close that he can yell back and slam the door when he leaves. But sometimes his stomach hurts in the morning.

They're getting up for work in the little houses and flats all across the old neighborhood known as Bridgeport, and thanks to the man for whom the limousine waits, about two thousand of the forty thousand Bridgeport people are going to jobs in City Hall, the County Building, the courts, ward offices, police and fire stations. It's a political neighborhood, with political jobs, and the people can use them. The ranks very low among the city and suburban communities in education. Those who don't have government jobs work hard for their money, and it isn't much. Bridgeport ranks low in income, too.

They're a blend of Irish, Lithuanian, Italian, Polish, German, and all white. It's a suspicious neighborhood. In the bars, heads turn when a stranger comes in. Blacks pass through in cars, but are unwise to travel by on foot. When a black college student moved into a flat on Lowe Avenue only a block north of the pink bungalow, there was a riot and he had to leave.

MORE

a prominent judge going into the office of Don Coe, the paper's straitlaced editorial writer. The city's mood was somewhat somber—the Cook County court system had just been rocked by the "Greylord" corruption scandal, the highlight film of which showed judges taking payoffs. Royko asked Gratteau, "What's Don doing?"

"Editorial boards for retention of judges," she replied. Royko's eyes gleamed. The timing was perfect. Once a month or so the columnist would organize a poker game in a downtown hotel room, and one was scheduled that day. Royko had several hundred dollars in cash in an envelope. He told Gratteau, "Wait till the judge leaves. Go in, hand it to Don, and say the judge said, 'This is for you.' " The judge left. Gratteau made the drop. A minute later a highly agitated Coe came running out of his office, cash spilling from the envelope, yelling, "Which way did he go? Which way did he go?"

Gratteau may have been the legman who knew Royko best. She met him in the summer of 1971 while working part-time as a copy clerk on the *Daily News*. A year later she interviewed him for a class project at the University of Illinois–Chicago Circle campus. They hit it off. Before long Gratteau was in the circle of friends who could drop by Royko's office just to hang out, smoke, and talk smart. "He had a little cubbyhole in the back," Gratteau recalls. "It was a little glass hut in the corner of the city room, overlooking the Chicago River. It had a desk with an overflowing ashtray. Boxes piled everywhere. I'd just go back there and knock a pile of crap off a chair. Mike always had his legs up on his desk, arms behind his head, glasses up on his forehead."

Royko encouraged her to go to work for the City News Bureau, as he had, to learn the streets. Late one afternoon her phone at City News rang.

"Gratteau?"

"Yeah."

"Royko."

"Uh-huh."

"You planning on staying in the business?"

"Yeah."

"Well, why don't you come to work for me?"

She did. Typically, Gratteau says, she'd arrive at the office around nine o'clock. "The phones would be ringing off the hook. A lot of the morning was spent fielding phone calls, sifting through a lot of stuff that came in, and figuring out what would work for Mike. What would make a good story for him to tell in his column—which was sometimes different than what a regular story was. So being Mike's legman required not only being a reporter but also being a kind of news editor."

Inevitably, once people learned she worked for Royko, they had a question: What's he really like? Her usual

reporting and gave him a memo, in story form, along with names and phone numbers at the top, of everyone you talked to, in case he wanted to follow up."

Eventually he would start writing. "He would take the memo," Gratteau says, "and turn it into something wonderful. Sometimes it was unrecognizable. Today in the newspaper business we have focus groups to figure out what readers want. Mike knew from the day he started writing to make people understand why this was important to them."

Sometimes in the office the phone would seem permanently wired to his ear. Studs Terkel once observed what it was like to watch Royko take a call at the paper: "He is listening. Some nobody is at the other end of the phone. Sometimes it's a cry for help. Sometimes it's an astonishing tip. Sometimes it's just a funny story. Other calls may come from some fat stuff with clout, whose venality he has exposed to the light. Always his response is a growl, more of a grunt. But don't let it fool you. He's not missing a beat."

A caller to the John Dempsey radio show in Chicago—on a program devoted to Royko after his death—related his experience of calling the columnist to inform him that the Illinois legislature had axed funding for school field trips for handicapped kids. Royko eventually wrote a column pointing out that the amount of

answer: "He's exactly like his columns. He can be bitingly funny, extremely sentimental, he was all of those things. On a day-to-day basis, you never knew which Mike was going to walk in the door."

When he did walk in, they'd have an informal meeting at his desk. Gratteau would have been through the mail and the phone messages. "You'd run down the possibilities. He'd say, 'Work on this. Don't work on this. I want this for later. I want this for today.' You did all the

Royko at a party with seven of his assistants—the leg people he called his "most valued friends."

Left to right: Hanke Gratteau, Terry Shaffer, Ellen Warren, Wade Nelson, Helene McEntee,

John Fennell, and Pat Wingert; with the chicken: the man they called "Mr. Big."

money that had been cut was about equal to what Illinois legislative leaders had just spent to commission oil portraits of themselves that would hang in the capitol.

The man remembered the phone call: "He was an amazing guy to talk to. He had a capacity to listen—it was eerie or frightening to call him. There would be a supernatural silence on the other end of the line. You'd be like at a confessional explaining yourself."

Yet those were probably the best calls. As Gratteau says, "Particularly at the *Daily News,* Mike would get tons of calls from ordinary people, the little guy up against the establishment."

One such tip led to a Royko classic. He was always infuriated by injustice, by bureaucrats who couldn't be bothered, and this one, well, Royko himself said later it "probably got the most public reaction." In December of 1973 he wrote about Leroy Bailey, a Connecticut man who in 1968 had been blinded and had most of his face blown off by a mortar shell in Vietnam. Back home the Veterans Adminstration did what it could, which wasn't much, and Bailey eventually wound up living in the basement of his brother's home in suburban Chicago, wearing a hood when he went out so he wouldn't frighten people.

"His family found a plastic surgeon who was doing some pioneering work," Royko said later. The doctor could reconstruct Bailey's face so he could at least eat solid food. Bailey underwent the surgery and submitted the bill to the VA. It was denied on grounds that Bailey's condition wasn't service related.

Royko's column hit the VA like a mortar shell. "The next day," Royko recalled, "[President] Nixon had a press conference and he opened the press conference by saying he had ordered the VA to take immediate steps" to take care of Bailey.

That and a number of other tough columns did not endear Royko to the VA. But when Royko's aged father, Mike Sr., needed full-time care, the columnist suggested to his brother and sisters that he go into a VA hospital. His brother Bob was doubtful. "After all the stuff you've written about them?" Mike nodded. "That's why."

Mike Sr. did well at the VA, but it's unlikely he duplicated the circumstances of his room at the YMCA, where he had lived previously. At the Y, this man who had lived hard his whole life suddenly developed a passion for fruit. Bob's sister Dorothy Zetlmeier called him in Wisconsin and said, "Daddy keeps asking me to bring him fruit, and more fruit. Isn't it wonderful?" Sure it was. The next time Dorothy visited she drew back a curtain in the corner of his room. Their father was operating a still.

Royko's tips came because of his high visibility as a columnist. That was the upside of fame—that and the money from *Boss* and his salary from the column, which naturally rose as his star did. The *Daily News* was desperate not to lose him, and when Royko's contract was up in 1971, the *Chicago Tribune* made the first of many attempts to lure him across Michigan Avenue to Tribune Tower. A *Tribune* limousine picked him up at the Billy Goat and took him out to a fancy restaurant in the suburbs, which said a lot right there about the differences between the two papers. Royko recalled, "It came as close as having the contract in front of me and the pen in my hand and I said, 'I can't do it.' I couldn't see myself working for the *Tribune*. All my life the hair on the back of my neck stood up when I read the *Trib*. They said I was crazy. I told them they were right. But I still couldn't do it."

But the *Daily News* gave him a raise, a big raise, and there was the book money, though the paperback distribution of *Boss* hit a few potholes, courtesy of Mayor Daley's wife, who got neighborhood stores to take it off the shelves. Other machine types originally kept it from being sold at the airport, though a reader wrote Royko at the *Daily News* suggesting it wasn't clout that kept *Boss* out of the airport, it was the fact the book "stinks." Royko answered: "Your theory may be perfectly valid, and I'm not blaming the mayor or the man who runs those concessions at the airport. Or even the man's wife, who is related to the mayor."

Of course Daley couldn't stop the book's runaway sales, and Royko and Carol used the money to buy a vacation cottage and to take a trip to Europe, with their kids, on a luxury liner. The cottage was on a lovely small lake in southeastern Wisconsin called Bohners Lake, just far enough from the tourist bustle of Lake Geneva. Carol's parents had owned a place in a wooded area near Bohners Lake for years. It was tiny, just a shell of a cottage, but Fred Duckman, who was an electrician and carpenter, had fixed it up, and Mike and Carol knew it well. The Duckmans sold it in 1969 when they moved out of the old funeral home on Central and Mike and Carol moved to Edgebrook. A few years later, when Royko was looking around the Lake Geneva area, nothing really grabbed him and he thought of Bohners Lake.

They got lucky. There was a place for sale that was perfect—a cedar house, surrounded by big trees, on land that sloped gently to the water. As soon as they tracked down the realtor, Royko wrote a check on the spot, and the summer home became a big part of their lives. Before the decade was out, it would be the setting for one of Royko's most poignant, heartwrenching columns.

But that was later. First, there were wonderful times. "They had found a great place," David Royko says. "It was really nice. That's where we actually were able to

spend time together. My father would take us water ski-ing, and we would really be a family."

Mostly it was just the family—Mike and Carol were a little selfish about it—but occasionally close friends were invited up. One of Mike's closest was John Sciackitano, a tall, burly native of Humboldt Park who worked in graphics and production at the *Chicago Sun-Times*. "I was up at Bohners Lake one Fourth of July," Sciackitano recalls, "and Mike was like a little kid, light-ing firecrackers, sticking pinwheels on trees. It was a real clear, starry night. We were out on the deck. Mike put the speakers under the deck and we sat on lawn chairs for hours, looking at the sky and listening to music."

They had met in 1972, on a weekend when they both were at work and Sciackitano spotted Royko in his *Daily News* office. "We have a mutual friend," Sciackitano said.

"Who?"

Sciackitano mentioned a kid from the old Humboldt Park neighborhood and Royko laughed. The kid was the neighborhood wimp. One day, being chased by a bully, he had run into Royko's house. Mike was about ten and the kid swept past him with the bully in pursuit. They ran into the Royko kitchen where Mike's mother, Helen, swatted the bully with a frying pan. All those years later at the newspaper, Royko and Sciackitano cracked up laughing. The wimp, as it turned out, had taken it as

Top **The home on Bohners Lake that Mike and Carol bought after the success of *Boss*.**

Bottom **Relaxing on the lake, Mike, with his arm around Carol, is driving the boat. Behind them are Carol's brother Bob Duckman** **and his wife, Barbara, who was the daughter of Mike Royko's sister Eleanor.**

an omen and signed up for a Charles Atlas course and become a bodybuilder.

Royko and Big Shack, as everyone called Sciackitano, became inseparable. Royko recruited Shack for the paper's softball team, and that meant, of course, a certain amount of postgame drinking at Billy Goat's. Late one night, driving home, Royko's foot was killing him. He became enraged at his shoe. Finally he rolled down his window and threw the shoe onto the expressway.

The next morning Royko called Shack before picking him up to drive to work.

"Shack?"

"Yeah, Mike."

"Do you have my shoe?"

"It's on the expressway, Mike."

A prolonged silence. "We'll look for it on the way in."

They shared an easy camaraderie, a distrust of pretense, a dislike of elitism. Once Shack was in Royko's office at the paper when the columnist opened a letter from Harvard University. They wanted to pay him several thousand dollars and all expenses to come and speak to their students. Royko tossed the letter, then looked at Sciackitano, who was teaching a journalism class himself at Roosevelt High School in Chicago.

"Aren't you ever going to ask me to come and talk to *your* students?"

Shack said no, he didn't think Mike would do it. "Well," Shack recalls, "he came to Roosevelt, and for three hours, with twenty-five young people sitting around, he talked about his career."

About the closest Royko may have come to pretense came in the late summer of 1972 when he and Carol took their boys to Europe, first class, aboard the SS *France*. They went to London, Monte Carlo, Munich, and Paris. Pretty rare air for a kid from Humboldt Park. Royko later claimed to have been in Maxim's, the famous Paris restaurant, and been offered an apéritif. "No," he said, "but I'd like a drink."

He also liked telling a story about the voyage. A blowhard in the ship's bar was voluntarily dispensing his worldview, and eventually he turned his attention to Chicago politics. The man's ignorance of the subject proved vast. Royko stood it for as long as he could, then said, "That's wrong. I'm from Chicago and that's wrong." The man said, "Your trouble is you don't understand Chicago politics, how it really works. There's a new book out by a guy named Mike Royko and if you read it, then you'll know."

At which point Royko grabbed the man's hand, shook it, and said, "My name is Mike Royko."

That was the fun of fame, of having a name people recognized, but there was a downside as well. For a time

To assist visitors I have prepared a primer on the mayor . . . Daley likes to build things. He likes high-rises, expressways, parking garages, municipal buildings and anything else that requires a ribbon-cutting ceremony and can be financed through federal funds. He isn't enthusiastic about small things, such as people. . . . In his parades, the politicians march up front. No matter how pretty they play, the flute players walk behind the horses.

it truly bothered Royko's oldest son, David. "I despised the question, 'Oh, are you related to Mike Royko?' " David says. "I hated being introduced to people as Mike Royko's son. More than half the time, people wouldn't even say the name Dave. Just, 'This is Mike Royko's son.' This was at a time when my own feelings about my father were kind of ambivalent, when I could see the effect his not being home was having on my mother."

David's younger brother, Rob, enjoyed it more, but he too found the coin of reflected fame to have two sides. Often it happened when producing his driver's license, which Robby, with a heavy foot as a teen, found himself doing with some regularity. "I was going ninety on Lake Shore Drive," Rob recalls. "The cop looks at my license. 'Royko? Go ahead, get out of here. You're lucky I'm letting you go.' " A similar situation on Lincoln Avenue had a less happy ending. "He was about to let me go," Rob recalls. "Then he said, 'You're not related to Mike Royko, are you?' I said, 'Yeah, he's my father.' Well, he gave me *five* tickets. Cracked windshield, headlamp off, going through a yellow—he was making stuff up. He threw them at me and said, 'Tell that Polack the whole police force hates his guts.' "

The columnist himself was now being recognized all the time, often in the bars where he went to unwind. The results varied. "If you came up to him and were polite and considerate," John Sciackitano said, "more often than not he was polite and considerate. If you came up to him and said, 'Hey, Royko, I read you yesterday and you don't know your ass from a hole in the ground,' then you were in trouble. The last thing you wanted was for Mike to call you 'chum.' That meant he was getting ready for battle."

Sciackitano told a story of being with Royko in a bar in suburban Niles that was owned by Carol's cousin. A handsome young couple had recognized Royko. The man quickly had a pen out for an autograph and was telling of his devotion as a reader. When he left to use the rest room, the young woman nuzzled close to the columnist and claimed to be an even bigger fan. Royko did not discourage her interest. Sciackitano, whose attention had been elsewhere, heard a commotion and turned around.

"The guy had Mike bent over the bar and was choking him. They called the police and I peeled his hands off Mike. When they were leading the guy out the door Mike yelled, 'Hey, jerk, I still have your pen.' "

Another episode from the mid-seventies, one that made the newspapers, ended with the police taking Royko away. The site was in a singles bar on Lincoln Avenue, not Royko's regular turf, and his buddies had gone home. Royko got into it with a group of people who turned out to be actors not averse to a little publicity once they found out the identity of their antagonist. During the exchange, ketchup spilled on a woman's coat, and it became the most famous clothing stain in Chicago history. "They made a big thing about the ketchup, and it drove me up a wall," Royko said. "They made me out as some kind of weirdo throwing ketchup at a woman."

The actors let it drag out, milking the publicity. "The woman's not the problem," Royko said at one point. "She's satisfied. I've written her a letter of apology. Christ, it's a collector's item. I said I was the worst piece of shit that ever lived. I groveled. We offered to buy her a new fur coat. She said she didn't need a new one, just pay for the cleaning on the old one. We did. It's the guys. They say, 'He behaved very badly. He was drunk.' Of course I was drunk. That's what I thought saloons were for." The case eventually did settle.

There were happier encounters. Dan Hurley, a Chicago contractor who became Royko's close friend and golfing buddy, remembers sitting with Royko at the Billy Goat on a Saturday morning, a time and day when the columnist was almost never at the bar he had made famous. "This girl from Michigan came in just to see if she could see Mike Royko," Hurley says. "She had her family with her. She sat down, her sister sat down, her boyfriend sat down, and Mike was just incredibly gracious. He signed some things for her. He told her boyfriend how lucky he was. When she walked out of there she was four feet off the ground. I'd never seen anybody so happy."

Royko always claimed to have never sought fame, and though he wasn't above using his name to get a restaurant table or meet a pretty girl, his claim seems accurate. He spurned the lecture circuit—and considerable riches—and almost never went on television, despite repeated requests. Royko once laughed that he held the record for saying no the most times to Ted Koppel's *Nightline*.

Royko explained: "The bad part of winding up as something I never wanted to be, and I try to avoid being— a celebrity journalist—is if you go somewhere to cover something, you wind up getting more attention than the person or event you're covering. . . . The first three years I had a column my picture wasn't in the paper. Number one: It isn't a very pretty picture. Number two: I didn't want people to know what I looked like."

He escaped the attention on his beloved softball diamonds and took some pride in having broken a leg in 1976 and *finishing the game.* "I play softball," he once said, "because if I hit a game-winning home run and I hoof it around the bases, I can kid myself into thinking I'm seventeen again." His off-hours also found him, increasingly, in fishing boats. Sciackitano takes credit for renewing Royko's interest in fishing. Royko had fished in the Humboldt Park pond as a kid, but once

he took it up again, he immersed himself in it, true to form. According to his son Rob, "When he got into fishing, he read a hundred books on fishing. Anything he did, he had to do it fifty times harder than the average person. Anything my father did, he did in total excess."

Royko went fishing in northern Wisconsin with Marshall Field, owner of the *Sun-Times* and the *Daily News,* and he and Sciackitano took fishing trips to Kentucky in the spring. Shack would buy the groceries and Mike would cook—Italian dishes were a specialty. Mostly, there were long days on the water. "I don't fish

Friends often said Royko seemed happiest in the hours after a softball game, relaxing with friends and teammates in a saloon.

to catch the fish so much as I really like . . . I like dawn on a lake," Royko said. "I like mists over a lake in the Ozarks. I like the way the air smells. I like the feeling of tiredness at the end of a long day of fishing."

Royko's stress level was not helped by the growing realization that the *Daily News*—the paper that had hired him when no one else would—was in serious financial trouble. It was hardly the only afternoon paper in the country with circulation woes, but Royko looked around the newsroom and saw gifted reporters and editors, friends he had grown up with in the business, and shook his head. It didn't make sense. They were putting out a good paper. They were having fun. It couldn't be coming to an end. Marshall Field put his top young editor, Jim Hoge, in charge of the *Daily News,* and Hoge gave Royko an editor's title and a bigger role in key editorial decisions—on top of writing his five columns a week, of course. In December of 1976, Richard J. Daley died. Royko wrote a surprisingly gracious column the next day, praising Daley for reflecting his city's rough-and-tumble strengths, criticizing his weaknesses, and chuckling over the political brawl sure to ensue as various pols scrambled to grab the throne.

...reds o...

...s to their hom...

...g set of lungs to prote...

...g of flunkies, has a full-ti...

...my ...remember a West side sto...

...n, and by the same guy, t...

...on a first-name basis. Whe...

...the grocer would bring ou...

...in the air before a word was

...rocer never had full...

...have a squa...

...ho co...

3

Success and Sorrow at the *Sun-Times*

There was nothing to chuckle about on March 4, 1978, when the *Daily News* published its final edition. The top line headline was "So Long, Chicago," and Royko wrote a goodbye column that ran on page one. The day before, he'd likened the folding to the soft summer evenings of his youth when the sun had disappeared but the kids all still wanted to play one more game of baseball. Just one more. But it wasn't to be.

Hoge, the editor, assumed his star columnist would join him at the *Sun-Times*. Royko wasn't so sure. There had never been a great deal of affection between the two staffs, though they shared a building. Royko would run off *Sun-Times* staffers who wandered into the *Daily News* city room. Now he was being asked to work with them. "I told Jim Hoge at the last minute I wasn't going to do it," Royko said. Hoge, however, reminded Royko that, in the days leading up to the *Daily News*'s demise, the columnist had lobbied strongly on behalf of two *Daily News* staffers for jobs at the *Sun-Times,* one in particular with a medical problem. Hoge had hired them. "He called in the marker," Royko said. Hoge asked for six months—he'd prove they could put out a hell of a paper. "It worked out better than I thought," Royko said. "Sixty or seventy people from the *Daily News* went over and we were really able to produce one of the best newspapers in the country."

Around this time Chicago politics, never dull, grew particularly lively. Royko, with more readers than ever, particularly in the city where the *Sun-Times* was strongest, was in the middle of every fray. The fallout from Daley's death continued, and in one memorable column Royko imagined some pretenders to the throne holding a seance. When the late mayor was contacted, he dismissed all the candidates, saying that even in his present condition he was the man for the job.

Royko's *Sun-Times* office looked
out over the Chicago River.

But it was a U.S. Senate race that may have best shown the tangible political power of Royko's column. Incumbent Republican Charles Percy, the millionaire former president of Bell and Howell, had embraced Washington a little too much for some tastes. Never a man of the people, Percy enjoyed the trappings of office more than getting around to meet his constituents, which is fine until you stand for reelection, which Percy did in the fall of 1978. Any decent Democrat would have had a shot, and Alex Seith, pretty much an unknown—a condition that served him well in the early going—took a startling lead in the polls.

Then Royko began filling in his readers on Seith. He was, the columnist said, little more than a standard machine hack, with shady friends and a not altogether altruistic outlook on public service. Seith's campaign grew

increasingly nasty, which Royko noted in a column recalling a couple of kids in his old neighborhood. One was Bad Russell, who "swore, smoked, said filthy things to girls. He shoplifted at the dime store, stole bikes, and stood under the L station steps so he could peek up ladies' skirts." The other kid was Nice Norbert, a decent and honest youngster who kept getting picked on by Bad Russell. It wasn't hard for readers to recognize Seith and Percy.

The columns seemed to energize the Percy campaign. They reprinted one as a full-page newspaper ad, which ran in the *Chicago Tribune* (the *Trib* must have loved that) under the headline "Before you vote, read Mike Royko." Illinois voters did, and Percy squeaked out a win. Did Royko swing the election? When Royko held his first Ribfest event a few years later in Grant Park, Percy was there.

Then there was Jane Byrne, an unknown, midlevel city bureaucrat with a quixotic plan to challenge Daley's successor, Michael Bilandic, for mayor in 1979. Byrne benefited from a series of Royko columns attacking Bilandic, particularly when the columnist seized on the pitiful performance by Chicago's street crews after the city was socked by a blizzard a month or so before the primary. The problem, Royko said, was that, while patronage appointees might go to great lengths to get out the vote and win elections, they rarely care to be bothered with trivialities, such as work.

"They are very good at what they do," Royko wrote. "But they're of little use when it comes to shoveling snow off the streets. . . . [Bilandic] couldn't very well admit that he can't ask good precinct captains to mess around with snow and ice. The salt might corrode their pinkie rings."

Charles Percy

Byrne's upset victory made headlines around the country, and the new mayor sent Royko a bronze placard inscribed with one word: "Boss." In May of 1979 *Esquire* magazine ran a lengthy profile of Royko under the title "The Man Who Owns Chicago."

It was a heady time, and then, with absolutely no warning, it all came crashing down. Carol Royko, the neighborhood girl Mike had loved since adolescence, suffered a cerebral hemorrhage and died on September 19, 1979, her husband's forty-seventh birthday. She had been vacationing in Florida and, their son Rob recalls, "was coming back from Florida to surprise my dad on his birthday." She was forty-four years old. Her husband was absolutely devastated. "No matter how hard people tell you it hit him," David Royko says, "nobody can exaggerate it. It's hard to believe he survived. I mean, it really is hard to believe. I guess having kids is maybe why he didn't jump off a bridge."

The column was suspended for the first and only time. Bob Royko brought his brother to the new home he and Geri had recently moved into in Bartlett, Illinois. The weeks there probably saved his life. Bob and Geri's young kids, Steve and Amelia—to whom Mike would later dedicate a book—clung to him. He'd have an arm around one while patting the other on the head.

At night, he drank—a lot. Mike would say, "Don't think I don't see you watering down my drinks," when Geri tried to make them a little lighter. Geri Royko, who takes guff from no one, would point out that it was her house, she was the boss, and Mike would smile. But it was the lowest point of his life. He talked of quitting the column. Young Steve Royko, going in to check on his uncle, who was sleeping in Steve's room, came downstairs and asked Geri why Uncle Mike had so much medicine on the nightstand. When Geri checked she found a great many pills, prescriptions for both Mike and Carol, and she flushed them down the toilet. Mike was upset. Geri said gently that she would not permit him to hurt himself in her house.

On October 5, three weeks after Carol's death, Royko's column appeared again in the *Sun-Times*. It was a personal letter to his readers, expressing his gratitude for the outpouring of support, and paying tribute to his late wife. Quite simply, he wrote, she was the best person he ever knew. He told his readers he needed a little more time to mend but he intended to be back. He ended the column by saying that if you have people you love, tell them so. Life is fragile. Tell them now.

Six weeks later, back at the paper full-time, Royko wrote another column about a man closing down a summer cottage for the last time. It was clearly his and Carol's place at Bohners Lake, and it was terribly sad.

But the emotional power of the prose was also a signal that maybe he was going to be all right.

Royko's sister Eleanor and her husband, Ed Cronin, moved into the house in Edgebrook to be with Rob and David. Robby in particular had always been the rebel, the one most likely to meet Slats Grobnik some night in a dark alley. With his mother's death, the wildness increased.

The patchwork family managed, but it wasn't easy. Too many ghosts. David said his father never again slept in the bed he'd shared with Carol. "And you know," David said, "my dad had a real love and knowledge of classical music. He'd mention it occasionally in his column, but even when he did it didn't show the depth of appreciation he had. But he stopped listening after my mom died. I think it hurt too much. There were a lot of things that changed after my mom died, and music was a big one." Along with grief, there was guilt, about the times he hadn't been home, about all the things he had intended to make up for in the future, now lost.

The healing process was helped in 1981 when Royko moved into a luxurious condominium at 3300 Lake Shore Drive. He bought a piano and began to play. John Sciackitano would stop by and find Mike deep into "Ain't Misbehavin'." Not surprisingly, he got a column out of the move to the lakefront. Walter Jacobson,

Chicago Sun-Times, Friday, February 26, 1982

Mike Royko wins Ernie Pyle award

Sun-Times columnist Mike Royko has won the $2,000 Ernie Pyle Memorial Award for outstanding human interest reporting, the Scripps-Howard Foundation announced.

Royko's works were selected from 300 newspaper entries submitted during 1981 as best exemplifying the warmth and craftsmanship of Pyle, a famous Scripps-Howard World War II correspondent and "people" columnist, according to Jacques A. Caldwell, the foundation's president.

"WITH unwavering honesty and straightforwardness," the contest judges said, "Mike Royko adroitly depicts ordinary people and ordinary places to turn Chicago into one of the great cityscapes of the modern journalistic world. His columns capture the mood and character of the Windy City in the way Chicagoans like to think of themselves: big and tough and yet with an abiding sense of humor and compassion for the little guy that was one of the trademarks of Ernie Pyle."

The contest was judged by Dr. Richard G. Gray, director of Indiana University's School of Journalism; Michael Grehl, editor, the Commercial Appeal, Memphis; and David Laventhol, publisher, Newsday, Long Island.

Royko previously won a Pulitzer Prize, a National Headliner Award and a Heywood Broun Award. Last year, he was named the first winner of the H. L. Mencken Award.

HE IS THE author of four books including the national best-seller, *Boss: Richard J. Daley of Chicago.*

Donald M. Williams, of the Miami Chief, Miami, Texas, was awarded second prize, $1,000 and a citation, in the 29th annual Pyle awards.

The judges awarded an honorable mention to John Arnold of the Miami (Fla.) Herald.

The winners will be honored at an April 7 luncheon in Cincinnati.

Congrats, Mike! We're all proud of you. Your pal, Slats.

GO with the **Sun-Times** It makes more sense

Although devastated by his wife's death, Royko continued pounding out award-winning columns.

a Chicago TV anchor and commentator who Royko claimed was paid more money per IQ point than anyone in journalism history, had knocked the columnist on the air for deserting the old neighborhood for a trendy condo. Royko responded with a hilarious column explaining that the move was part of a lifelong study in social anthropology. Royko pointed out that he'd lived in flats and bungalows and could easily report on that culture, but lakefront condo creatures, with their jogging, bottled water, and cappuccino machines, needed closer study.

It may be that the always-daunting task of turning out five columns a week of consistently high quality helped Royko. It gave him a center, and he threw himself into the job harder than ever. The columns of that time were marvelous, among his best. Royko was elected to the Chicago Journalism Hall of Fame in 1980, and in 1981 the *Baltimore Sun* selected him for the first H. L. Mencken Writing Award, calling the columnist's work "witty, biting, irreverent, stylistically graceful." A year later Royko received the Ernie Pyle Award for outstanding human interest reporting.

Royko's fourth collection of columns, *Sez Who? Sez Me,* published in 1982, made a number of national best-seller lists, and the reviews confirmed Royko's emergence as the top newspaper columnist in the country. The *Albuquerque News* wrote: "Newspaper columnists fall into five general categories. The categories, in ascending order, are: 1) Bad. 2) Good. 3) Very good. 4) Outstanding. 5) Mike Royko. And that, as they say, is that. Royko is the best; nobody comes close to Royko; God only made one Royko and that's too bad."

The subject of one of the columns in *Sez Who? Sez Me* might have disagreed with that assessment. Frank Sinatra had come to Chicago in May of 1976 for a series of concerts and established as his base the penthouse suite at the luxurious Ambassador East Hotel. No problem there, except that Royko found out that the Chicago police were providing Sinatra with a uniformed guard at the door of the suite twenty-four hours a day. Royko wrote a tough, funny column wondering why a big shot like Sinatra, with all his flunkies, deserved armed protection when ordinary Chicago taxpayers barely rated "getting scraped off the sidewalk after somebody has bashed them in the head."

Sinatra was not amused, but rather than do the smart thing and ignore it, he chose to start a feud, which immediately earned Royko's gleeful participation. The

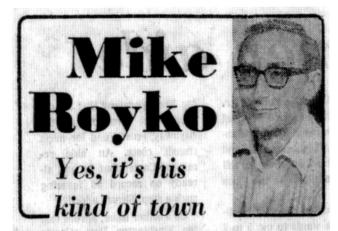

Mike Royko

Yes, it's his kind of town

Every eight hours, a policeman leaves the Chicago Av. police station and goes to the Ambassador East Hotel. He rides the elevator to the penthouse. There he relieves another policeman who was standing in the hallway.

For the next eight hours, he will be there in the hallway, guarding the entrance to the suite.

When his shift ends, another policeman will show up and take his place.

This goes on 24 hours a day, 7 days a week.

AND WHO ARE THEY GUARDING? A witness in a big murder case? A high government official?

Why, it's Ol' Blue Eyes, as he is called in the gossip columns, that's who.

Yes, while ordinary Chicagoans are running for their lives from each other, triple-locking their own doors, and counting on luck and maybe a watchdog to keep the fiends from their throats, Frank Sinatra rates a cop right outside his door as long as he's in town to sing at a nightclub.

Every night, hundreds of scrub ladies make it from their downtown jobs to their homes, with only a heavy purse and a strong set of lungs to protect them. But Sinatra, with his army of flunkies, has a full-time police guard.

I remember a West Side storekeeper who was robbed so often, and by the same guy, that he and the stickupman were on a first-name basis. When the robber walked in the door, the grocer would bring out the money and put his hands in the air before a word was said.

The grocer never had full-time police protection. He was lucky to have a squad car drive by once in a while. But Sinatra, who could probably hire a Brink's truck to fetch his salami sandwiches, has somebody nearby while he's sleeping.

WE ASKED THE COMMANDER of the district why a full-time guard is assigned to Sinatra. He said he's not sure. The order came from downtown.

Deputy Supt. Sam Nolan bucked the question to David Mozee, who is director of news affairs for the department. Mozee said:

"Sinatra and his people asked for police protection because of some threats he received."

Wow! Threats are news. From who? Gamblers? Mobsters? Some disgruntled girl who had wanted to be introduced to Sam Giancana or Jack Kennedy?

"They were anonymous phone calls."

There are women in this city who regularly hear from panters, breathers, grunters and other assorted lewd commentators. Cops don't plant themselves outside the doors of these women. They say: "Just hang up, lady."

But some drunk with 20 cents, who doesn't like the way Ol' Blue Eyes parts his hairpiece, can make a phone call, and the Chicago Police Department takes it seriously.

Mozee continued:

"We feel that we owe him protection. He's a noted person, and he's liked and disliked."

WELL, I HATE TO BRAG, BUT I THINK that around here, I'm every bit as disliked as Sinatra. But I wouldn't think of asking for a police guard. He'd probably dislike me, too, so what's the advantage?

If being noted and disliked were grounds for having a cop outside the door, half the police department would be tied up guarding TV weathermen, sportscasters, columnists, liberal aldermen, independent candidates for mayor and Cub pitchers.

Mozee said another reason Sinatra rates special treatment is that he is going to appear at a police ceremonial event while he is performing here.

"It's customary for the police department to provide anyone who comes in town to do something for us with protection."

That's nice. But a lot of people do things for the police—such as paying the taxes that pay their salary. And that barely rates them getting scraped off the sidewalk after somebody has bashed them in the head.

FRANKLY, I'M SURPRISED that Sinatra, who has such a tough reputation, would need somebody standing outside at all hours. He's an absolute terror when it comes to punching out elderly drunks or telling off female reporters.

Besides, he's a friend of the late Sam Giancana, former boss of the Chicago syndicate, and in Chicago that ought to mean something.

And maybe it does.

singer sent Royko a registered letter, which the columnist reprinted the next day. He apologized to Sinatra for saying the singer had flunkies. Why, Royko said, I'll even apologize to the flunky who delivered the letter.

That night at his concert, Sinatra fanned the flames: "At least we didn't invite Jerko or whatever his name is,"

Sinatra told his audience. "Do you know he was our lookout at Pearl Harbor? I'd like to hire Chicago Stadium and box him for charity. We'll pay him a thousand dollars for every round he lasts. He won't make two dollars."

This inspired a third Royko column about a call he'd received from his old friend Ben Bentley, a Chicago fight promoter who had staged bouts for Rocky Marciano and Muhammed Ali. Bentley suggested that if Royko and Sinatra went at it in the north end zone of Soldier Field, he could sell twenty-five thousand tickets at fifty dollars apiece. Royko reluctantly turned him down, explaining, "I had never considered it civilized or gentlemanly to settle differences by fistfighting. My mother taught me that years ago. She said: 'Son, a gentleman does not soil his hands that way. If someone picks a fight with you, just ignore him. Then hire a couple of out-of-towners to break his legs.' "

Royko's beloved Cubs were also much on his mind. He never seemed bothered that they always found a way to snatch defeat from the jaws of victory. That was to be expected, and their bumbling provided material for his annual quiz on team history, which was always widely quoted in the city. The Cubs, Royko said, had always been "a triple-threat team. They are a threat to lose pitching, hitting or fielding."

But before the 1980 season began, the columnist, dismayed by what he called the "petulant jerks" and "cry babies" on the Cubs, decided to switch his allegiance. It was really his way of expressing his disgust with the growing arrogance of pro athletes in general. Royko got a column out of it by taking an oath declaring himself a White Sox fan on the pitcher's mound at Comiskey Park with his hand on the wooden leg of Sox owner Bill Veeck. Showing his level of seriousness, he switched back the next year. "I may change again before the year is out," he said. "Who knows what might happen some slow Thursday?"

There was one way to make the Cubs better—buy them. The plot, which came dangerously close to fruition, was hatched in the Billy Goat Tavern. Where else? Royko was drinking with an out-of-town friend, Charlie Finley, the colorful former owner of the Oakland A's. Finley mentioned to Royko that he'd heard the Wrigley heirs were looking to

Frank Sinatra

sell the Cubs. Estate taxes had hit them hard and they weren't going to sell the mother ship, the gum company, but the baseball team was another matter. "I think they can be bought for about $21 million," Finley said.

Royko brought it up to *Sun-Times* owner Marshall Field, with whom he had a fairly close friendship, and started urging him to buy the Cubs. "I said you can take it away from Channel 9, put it on Channel 32 [which Field owned at the time] and see if Channel 9 had enough old Charlie Chan movies to fill all that air time."

They took a fishing trip around that time, and Royko was relentless. "I wouldn't let up the whole four or five days we were fishing," the columnist said. "I came up with the idea we'd change the name of Wrigley Field to Field Field. Or Marshall Field. Whatever he wanted. I finally persuaded him it was a good idea."

Field's business advisors were dubious—"Oh, were they stupid," Royko said—but he went forward. Royko recalled, "Charlie was going to own five percent, I was going to own half of one percent, and Marshall was going to own 51 percent, controlling interest. Charlie Finley was going to find some reputable people for the rest. Charlie was out there hustling and pretty well had it put together, but then the tarpon started running. Marshall Field is a fanatic fisherman. If the tarpon were running, Marshall had to be there. He went off to Florida to catch tarpon."

With Finley on the street hustling investors, it didn't take long for word to get to the *Chicago Tribune*'s savvy and well-connected lawyer, Don Reuben. One morning Royko arrived at his office at the *Sun-Times* and someone said, "Did you hear about the Cubs?"

"What about 'em?"

"The *Tribune* just bought them."

Other adventures had happier outcomes. Royko had always taken pride in his ability to cook barbequed ribs. Friends from the paper often spent long summer weekends relaxing at a lake home owned by the family of Wade Nelson, one of his assistants, and at some point the columnist would dazzle those assembled with his ribs. Eventually Royko did a column, tongue firmly in cheek, claiming his recipe dated back to a rib joint run by his ancestors in seventeenth-century Warsaw. Letters poured in, many from blacks, good-naturedly insisting there was no way a honky like Royko could make decent ribs.

The gauntlet had been thrown down. Hanke Gratteau, no longer Royko's assistant but still at the paper and still his close friend, remembered being on vacation and taking the newspaper down to the pool. What she read made her nearly choke on her coffee.

"Mike had invited all of Chicago to Grant Park to cook ribs!" Gratteau dashed back up to her apartment and got

Well, I hate to brag, but I think that around here I'm every bit as disliked as Sinatra. But I wouldn't think of asking for a police guard. He'd probably dislike me, too, so what's the advantage? If being noted and disliked were grounds for having a cop outside the door, half the police department would be tied up guarding TV weathermen, sportscasters, columnists, liberal aldermen, independent candidates for mayor, and Cubs pitchers.

"Royko's Ribfest" drew thousands of Chicagoans to Grant Park in the early 1980s, including his adoring niece, Amelia, looking up with the glasses.

on the phone to her old boss. "Do you realize what you've done? This is enormous! Have you talked to the Park District? Have you done this? Have you done that?"

When she ran out of gas, Royko said, "Oh, we can do this."

And they did. "It was a wonderful event, just fabulous," Gratteau said. Chicago writer and Royko buddy Rick Kogan was chief judge. Mayor Byrne attended, but the true measure of success was the thousands of regular Chicagoans who came to enjoy the sunshine and the splendid smell of smoked pork wafting over the lakeshore. The contest was won by an avid amateur named Charlie Robinson who used his victory to launch rib restaurants bearing his name.

Royko liked the fun and unpretentious feel of that first Ribfest, and when he went looking to join a golf club, he wanted the same atmosphere. He may have seemed more like a public links golfer, but anyone who wants to play the public links in a big city has to get up about four in the morning and stand in line for a round that could take six hours to play. The club Royko found, Ridgemoor, had members who were the kind of people he was most comfortable with, self-made businessmen, first- and second-generation immigrants, people who knew about hard work, life, and loss and also knew how to have fun.

"The night we interviewed Mike for membership, he was very shy," recalls Dan Hurley, a Chicago-area contractor born in Ireland in 1929, who became one of Royko's best friends. "I'd been at a lot of interviews. There were guys who came in and gave you the feeling they were thinking, 'You're lucky I'm here.' Mike wasn't like that. He was quiet. He just answered the questions he was asked."

As part of the membership committee, Hurley would sometimes hear from established members about new applicants. They'd had high-profile members before— Congressman Dan Rostenkowski and Cubs broadcaster Jack Brickhouse were members at Ridgemoor—people who might cause a stir, but with Royko, Hurley said he only heard from one politico. "There was a politician-type who solicited me to keep Mike out of the club. Mike made politicians nervous. But I had taken to him right away. I knew damn well this was a good man."

The committee also sent out a letter to the general membership, asking for comment on prospective members, and the only letter in response to Royko's application asked if there had been any letters. When the board of directors vote at Ridgemoor, they put a black or white ball in a box. Two black balls and you're out. Royko got no black balls. The membership, it turned out, liked having a celebrity in its midst.

Royko's columns helped elect Jane Byrne mayor, and early in her administration they were friendly, as her appearance at an early Ribfest demonstrates. Later, Royko's tough columns on the people Byrne surrounded herself with angered the mayor, and their friendship cooled.

"They all knew Mike was there," Hurley says. "They all wanted to be in his circle. They'd look for an excuse to be around him. They'd come over and talk to me, hoping to get next to Mike. Mike once said to me, 'Danny, what's going on? Are you the greeter at this club? Everybody says hello to you.' "

They'd played their first round together a few weeks after Royko interviewed with the membership committee. It was a cold, dreary day, and Hurley spotted a solitary figure on the range, beating balls. As he approached, Hurley recognized Royko. "Are you enjoying the club?" he asked. They wound up playing a few holes together, and Royko said, "I might be playing next Monday. Interested?" The columnist brought Jim Warren, a reporter at the paper, and they had a good time. Hurley was impressed with Royko's golf knowledge. Before joining, Royko had walked the course, while there was snow on the ground, to make sure he approved of the routing of holes. "Mike was a very accomplished golfer in the service," Hurley says. "When he was up there around Seattle, he used to play every day. He told me that at that time he was around a five handicap." Taking the game up again, Royko quickly established a respectable handicap in the low double digits.

Of their friendship, Hurley says, "It just happened. We kind of grew on each other. We played every Sunday, and some Saturday afternoons." Often they'd partner, some-times in club events like the annual Thanksgiving "turkey trot" tournament. One year the weather was especially cold, and Royko, always looking for an edge, had a plan. "He came up with this idea," Hurley remembers, "that if the ball was warm, it would play a little better. He got a little thermos, and he got boiling water, and he put a dozen Titleists in there. He had fishnet to get the balls out. It was like he was boiling eggs. We get to the tee, it's bitter cold, and Mike fishes out a ball and proudly puts it on the tee. Everybody fell down laughing. The paint had peeled off the ball."

Royko made sure that every game included a wager of some sort. The columnist was a great short putter. Hurley recalls, "I said to him, 'Mike, if my life depended on it and I had somebody to make a five-foot pressure putt for me, you'd be my guy.' "

Royko snorted. "That's not pressure. Let me tell you what pressure is. Pressure is when it's six forty-five, and I have a seven o'clock deadline and I don't have a goddamn thought in my head."

It was one of his few public allusions to the exhausting nature of his life's work. There are a lot of jokes about the life of a daily columnist—it's like being married to a nymphomaniac because as soon as you're done you have to start over again. Only when it's happening to you, and your standards are such that you have become

Operation Angel vignette 12/20/78

Farewell, my ugly. . .

Mike Royko

They say that real-life private detectives don't have the kinds of adventures that fictional private eyes do, that most of their work is routine.

I'm not sure about that. One of Philip Marlowe's best-known cases, "Farewell, My Lovely," began routinely. He was looking for a runaway girl. Then he met big, ugly, mean Moose Malloy and suddenly he was off on a runaway thriller.

Something quite similar happened recently to Scott Rogers, 22, who is beginning his career as a private eye for a security service.

Most of the time, his job consists of looking around apartment house hallways and shaking knobs on factory doors.

But a few nights ago, he was out on the street working on a case. Like Philip Marlowe, he was looking for a teen-aged girl who had run away from home.

He had tracked her down once before so he went back to the same neighborhood on the Near North Side where he knew she had some seamy friends.

HE FIGURED he'd check out the bars and talk to some street people he knew.

He was driving along slowly when he spotted two women who were just standing on the sidewalk near the curb. Since they weren't at a bus stop, and it was 10 o'clock at night, he was sure they weren't waiting for Halley's Comet.

So, as Rogers tells it, he stopped his car, leaned out the car window, and and started a conversation with one of the women that went something like this:

"Hiya."

"Hiya."

"I'm looking for someone."

"Who?"

"A girl."

At that moment, the second woman turned around and Rogers found himself looking into the barrel of a pistol.

He also was looking into one of the ugliest faces he had ever seen.

"It was a guy, with lipstick and rouge and a woman's wig. I mean, he wasn't a good-looking guy. He was tough looking. And with all that makeup and the wig, he was really something awful. And he was pointing a gun in my face."

I'm not sure what Philip Marlowe would have done at that moment. Probably quipped: "Who's your hairdresser, pal?"

BUT ROGERS couldn't think of anything to say. He just sat there, looking at that ugly face and the gun and feeling his blood drain toward his feet. Was he going to be murdered? If so, why? He resisted the urge to scream. Or to faint.

The ugly face said: "You're under arrest."

"Huh?"

"Get out of the car. You're under arrest."

Rogers got out of the car, feeling momentary gratitude that he wasn't going to be murdered. But he also felt indignant that he was being arrested.

"What are you arresting me for?" he said.

The ugly face pointed to the woman and said: "Soliciting. She's a police officer."

That's right. Rogers had been caught in the big round-up of hookers and their customers that took place over the weekend on the North Side.

In one of the funniest police operations in memory, called Operation Angel, more than 100 cops—many of them males dressed like women—posed as street-walking prostitutes. Then they arrested anyone who sought their charms.

In all, they arrested about 300 men, as well as about 30 prostitutes.

As he stepped from his car, Rogers said: "But I'm a private investigator."

"**SHUT UP**" said ugly face, pointing the gun at his belly.

Rogers said a policeman in uniform was standing nearby laughing.

"I told him I was a private investigator. I showed him my ID card. But he just said: 'Don't worry, kid, this is all just bull---- anyway."

So a paddy wagon pulled up and Rogers was shoved inside. And he began a journey that, he says, was the most bizarre of his young life.

"Every few minutes the wagon would stop and they'd put someone in—either a hooker or their customers. It got really crowded.

"Guys were yelling: 'I'm going to sue the city for this!' They were really shook up.

"Then the the hookers started yelling. 'We got to raise bond money. So we're charging half price.' "

Half price for what?

"Uh, you know," said Rogers. "For sex."

Sex in the back of a police paddy wagon?

"You bet. We were really packed in there. But guys were taking them up on it. You can't imagine the things that were going on!

"And there we were, going down Lake Shore Dr., and guys were having sex with the hookers, and some people were snorting cocaine and smoking marijuana. Boy, I never saw a sight like that in my life."

Didn't the police know what was going on?

"**ONE OF THEM** turned around and looked back, but he didn't say anything. I guess they just wanted to deliver us to the police station and didn't care."

Rogers sat in a cell awhile, then made bond. A couple of days later, he went to court and was ready to indignantly tell his story to the judge.

But the case was dropped because the policewoman didn't show up. Neither did the cop in drag who had arrested him.

"Too bad," said Rogers, finally sounding like a private eye. "I was kind of curious to see if he was uglier as a man or as a woman."

the very best, maybe the best there has ever been, it's not so very funny.

"He had, at best, what, a couple of hours' peace a day?" said Hanke Gratteau, his three-time assistant. "You've got one in, and you can savor that for a little bit before it starts gnawing on you that there's tomorrow, and the next day, and the day after that. It was the monster that ate him up. It took a toll on his health. It took a toll on his personal life. We're all the richer for it as readers, but what he sacrificed to make it happen is unbelievable."

When Gratteau got married, Royko insisted that the reception be at Ridgemoor, his new club. It was a beautiful day and there was a lovely sit-down dinner. But, of course, a lot of their mutual friends were newspaper people. Drinks were served at the reception. Royko was a bit nervous about how his fellow members would receive his friends, so he took a second drink. Things seemed to be going fine, Hanke was radiant, so he took a seat at the bar upstairs. Down by the pool, Rick Kogan, journalist and provocateur, noticed a colleague standing by the edge. Would Kogan push him in? Of course he would. "He seemed a little put out," Kogan says, "so to make him feel better I jumped in as well."

They got out of the pool, and Kogan, dripping wet, went upstairs and sat next to Royko. The columnist was furious.

"You know what just happened?"

"No," Kogan said. "What?"

"The greenskeeper just came by," Royko said, "and told me there are people throwing each other in the pool. Goddamnit, I'm going to be kicked out of this club!"

Kogan wiped a little water off his face and said, "Gee, Mike, do you want me to try to find out who it was?"

Royko's membership survived. Back at the paper, the column often dealt with national issues, reflecting his increasing popularity outside Chicago. When Ronald Reagan was elected president in 1980, Royko harpooned him at will, often using a scene from a movie—Royko was a dedicated film buff—to make his point. He'd suggest Reagan, the former actor, sometimes wasn't sure if he was in the Oval Office or on a movie set.

Chicago politics, ever more polarized, wasn't as much fun as it had been when he had the Machine to kick around, but there was one landmark mayor's race that Royko couldn't ignore. Before the 1983 election was over, Royko devoted more than fifty columns to it. First he dispatched Jane Byrne, pointing out that while she had initially run as a reformer, Byrne surrounded herself with people who raised obscene amounts of money for reelection campaigns and did little else other than insist on their share of the spoils.

Legislation and court rulings had torpedoed Chicago's

vaunted patronage machine—you could no longer hire and fire for political reasons—so incumbent pols turned their efforts to raising cash for TV commercials that would tell the electorate how hard they were working when in fact they were working on raising money to produce the commercials.

Byrne lost a three-way primary to black Congressman Harold Washington—the other loser was Cook County State's Attorney Richie Daley, son of Richard J. Daley. Chicago had never had a black mayor, so Republicans, sensing a chance for an unprecedented upset, rallied behind Bernard Epton, a wealthy lawyer and former state legislator who had a reputation as something of a liberal but made the mistake of running radio ads that said: "Epton—before it's too late." The meaning behind that kicker line wasn't hard to guess, and Royko hammered Epton for it and other stupidities, leading Epton to announce his plans to buy the *Sun-Times* so he could fire

Royko. That only led to another column, in which Royko called Epton's law firm and persisted in asking a confused receptionist if the firm was for sale, because the columnist wanted to buy it.

Royko also went after Harold Washington, and in doing so found out racial matters in the closing years of the century were subject to subtle manipulation. It began when Royko wrote a column wondering why Washington had failed to file four years of income tax returns.

"I liked Harold and Harold liked me," Royko said later. "But Harold had never answered to my satisfaction, and I don't think to anybody's satisfaction, why . . . he didn't bother to file returns."

When Washington survived the primary, Royko said, "I wrote a column that was not hostile. It was very straightforward. All that column said was that you should really explain this. He immediately said that if we have rioting in Chicago, it's because of Royko."

The columnist was stunned. "I thought, 'My God in heaven, what a reaction!' Jim Hoge [the *Sun-Times* editor] saw him [Washington] that night and said, 'Do you really think that was a racist column?' Harold said, 'Mike had to write what he has to write and I have to say what I have to say. He knows that.' It was a game. I felt a little bad about that. I would rather he said that I should

Jane Byrne
Harold Washington

explain why *I* didn't pay taxes one year. I'd rather have him do that than say I'm going to cause the city to be burned down."

The day after Washington won, Royko wrote a column saying he had told his Uncle Chester to relax, Washington didn't want to marry his sister. It was pitch-perfect, focusing on the new mayor's talents, ridiculing racial polarity, and finally saying that if everyone could keep a sense of humor, the city would be much better off.

Royko may have been a bit easier on Washington than earlier mayors, but the pilot fish who surround any newly successful politician did not escape the columnist's wrath. "It was amateur night," Royko said. "Harold brought in a lot of his people, who had never had access to that kind of power and that kind of opportunity before." They went for the spoils and in Royko's judgment were not very adept. "Theft of any kind, whether you're a burglar, a hijacker, a bank robber or embezzler, it takes certain basic skills. . . . You've got to learn your

Rupert Murdoch

trade. Harold's people who got caught were violating every rule of graft-taking. Never take anything from somebody you don't know. The big sting that the feds ran, my goodness, here was this absolute stranger and they were taking bribes from him. Tom Keane [a Daley crony] wouldn't have even gone in the same restaurant with a bozo like that."

For most of Washington's tenure as mayor, Royko's jabs and jibes did not appear in the *Sun-Times*. The rumor had first surfaced in 1983: Rupert Murdoch, the Australian media baron notorious for papers in England that featured screaming headlines and topless women, was making inroads in the United States. Now word had it that he was interested in the *Sun-Times*. Establishment Chicago—not to mention most everyone at the paper—was aghast. The *Sun-Times* was a tabloid but one with pizazz anchored in solid reporting.

At first no one seemed to believe Marshall Field would sell to Murdoch. Field told Jim Hoge—by then publisher—that he was talking to the Australian just to get an idea of market price. But Marshall's half-brother, Ted Field, wanted to sell, and there were whispers that Marshall had come to resent the popular Hoge, even as he moved him up at the paper.

The paper was perceived as Hoge's, and Field wanted out. Hoge put together a local group to give Field an alternative to selling to Murdoch. By that point Field was deep in negotiation with Murdoch, but apparently it wasn't too late. December 15, 1983, was a key

I can never really get mad at liberals, because they're so warm-hearted. They really want everybody to be happy. They want everything to be just right. Except it's never going to happen. . . . And if you really try to remake the whole society to make everything right, you're going to screw it up worse than it is now. . . . If a guy is really short, and I can't call him short, he ain't going to get any taller. I don't want to refer to people in a derogatory way. But let's be realistic about it. I guess I'm follicle-challenged. Don't call me bald! I don't think most people think that way.

One of Royko's enduring passions was
16-inch softball. He said he loved it
because when he hit a home run he
could feel like a teenager again.

date. Hoge was told that if a deal wasn't signed by then, all offers were again viable.

The day came and went without a sale, and Hoge's group asked Royko, Field's fishing buddy, to call the owner in Palm Beach. In a conference call on December 16, when Field said he was afraid Murdoch would take him to court, Hoge's group assuaged his fears. They would defend any suit.

Hoge had nagging doubts. He got back in touch with Royko, asking him to call Field again in Palm Beach for reassurance. This time Marshall couldn't be reached. Maybe the tarpon were running. Or maybe the game was over. On December 17, the sale of the *Chicago Sun-Times* to Rupert Murdoch was announced to the public.

Royko was furious, with Field, with Newton Minow, the Chicago lawyer and power broker who had represented Field in the deal, and maybe with what he now knew he had to do. He couldn't work for Murdoch. That left one daily newspaper in Chicago.

"I always thought of the *Tribune* as a great, big, humorless mausoleum," Royko said. "The *Tribune* guys all wore fedoras and looked very grim. They weren't having any fun."

His problems with the *Tribune* dated back to growing up in the Blue Sky Lounge. "The *Tribune* wasn't very popular in that neighborhood. Roosevelt's picture was never

taken from my father's wall. You had Custer's Last Stand and Roosevelt's picture. That was the artwork on one wall. There weren't any Republicans. I didn't meet a Republican until I was almost an adult. You just didn't have them."

Neither was Royko, as a young reporter, impressed with his early personal contacts with *Tribune* journalists. Royko and Carol had been at a political function in Springfield in the early sixties when the *Tribune*'s political editor approached them and began laying into Royko for something he'd written. "My wife tried to get him to go away," Royko recalled. "She knew I could be easily provoked. So he insulted my wife, and I sort of lost my temper. I picked him up and was going to throw him out a window. Fortunately, some people prevented it."

The *Tribune* political editor was a powerful man in Springfield. But what happened the next day was indicative of his and the paper's arrogance. "I was sitting in the press gallery," Royko said, "overlooking the Illinois House, and this line began forming. It was most of the state legislature, coming by to shake my hand. It was the most wonderful thing they'd ever heard of."

By 1984 the *Tribune* had changed, and for Royko, the changes could be seen as good and bad. With the death of Colonel Robert R. McCormick in 1955, the paper gradually grew less staunchly conservative, the journalists more professional and less ideological. It was a big change,

A Florida fishing vacation.

The Royko men: Bob, Rob, Mike, David, and in front, Bob's son Steve.

akin to turning around an ocean liner that had been on the same course for decades. The other change, less happy for someone like Royko, was also the indirect result of McCormick's death. McCormick was conservative and eccentric, but he was a newspaper guy, one of the last of the press barons. With him gone, the natural drift of the *Tribune* was to be less a newspaper and more like IBM or General Motors. Diverse, hugely profitable, faceless, noncontroversial.

When Murdoch's purchase of the *Sun-Times* seemed inevitable, Royko debated what to do. "I wasn't sure I was going to stay in newspapering," he said. "I gave some thought to just quitting, period. At the time I wasn't married, so I could have done that. I could have maybe done books. I thought about maybe going to another part of the country." Ben Bradlee at the *Washington Post* had been lobbying Royko hard to move to the nation's capital.

In the end, he went to the *Tribune*. "The day Rupert Murdoch took possession [of the *Sun-Times*]," Royko said, "I came in in the morning, dragged his new publisher out of his office, and handed him my resignation. Then I just walked across the street, had my lawyer meet me, and we went in."

Tower of the *Tribune*

4

The *Trib*'s editor was Jim Squires, who had let it be known that if Royko wanted to come, he was welcome. "I asked to see Jim Squires. I gave him my contract from the *Sun-Times,* and said change the name to the *Tribune,* I'll come here for the same terms. They just retyped it. They fixed me up with a place to work and I wrote a column that day."

Oddly enough, the next day Royko's column appeared in both the *Sun-Times* and the *Tribune*. The *Sun-Times* reprinted an old one, and Murdoch brought a lawsuit claiming the columnist was still under contract. Royko beat the "Alien," as he had taken to calling Murdoch, in court, because his *Sun-Times* contract had a fifteen-day resignation window in the event the paper was sold. Mike Royko was at the *Tribune,* in the most prestigious part of the paper, flush left down the side of page three, Monday through Friday.

If his professional life was now settled, Royko's personal life was also on the verge of calming down. There had been many dark days—not to mention nights—after Carol's death. "Our socializing at some point became more than just socializing," Hanke Gratteau said. "There was caretaking going on. I was awakened, on more than one occasion, by the [city] desk, saying, 'We just got a call from Joe Blow, the bartender at the Stop and Drink. You need to go get him out of there.' "

"It was a real desperate loneliness that was motivating him," Rick Kogan says. "He was at loose ends."

The better nights usually ended at a restaurant and piano bar called the Acorn on Oak. Royko loved the entertainer, Buddy Charles, who had grown up in Chicago and played great jazz piano.

Mostly they'd just sit and listen to Charles—but not

Tribune Tower. Royko worked here after beating a lawsuit to keep him at the *Sun-Times*.

Royko wins ruling in contract dispute
Sun-Times suit dismissed

By Joseph R. Tybor
Legal affairs writer

A COOK COUNTY circuit judge ruled Thursday that columnist Mike Royko is free to write for The Tribune.

Judge Anthony Scotillo ruled in favor of a motion made by The Tribune and joined in by Royko to dismiss a lawsuit filed Wednesday by the Chicago Sun-Times, which sought to prevent Royko from writing for The Tribune.

"It's one for the good guys," Royko said minutes after the ruling. "I'm delighted."

It was not immediately known whether the Sun-Times, which was purchased from Field Enterprises last Monday by Australian publishing magnate Rupert Murdoch, would appeal Scotillo's ruling.

"That's a decision that has to be made after people at the company consider it very carefully," said William P. Richmond, attorney for the Sun-Times.

Officials at the Sun-Times and The Tribune declined comment on the ruling. But E. Leonard Rubin, Royko's attorney, said, "I'm delighted, I'm tickled, I'm overjoyed."

"THE RULING MEANS that Mr. Royko is free to work for The Chicago Tribune and neither Mr. Royko nor The Chicago Tribune has done anything but act legally and properly," Don H. Reuben, attorney for The Tribune, said immediately after the ruling. "His right to work is no longer in dispute."

Pending a possible appeal by the Sun-Times, the ruling brings to an end a three-day mini-drama in which the two newspapers battled over which of them would get the highly paid services of one of the nation's best-known local columnists.

Scotillo's ruling followed his refusal Wednesday to issue a preliminary injunction that the Sun-Times had sought to prevent Royko from writing his column for The Tribune until the lawsuit could be heard.

Royko's column, which he has written since 1963, first for the Chicago Daily News and later for the Chicago Sun-Times, "parodied the foibles of the urban bureaucracy [and] has achieved a unique identity," according to the complaint filed by the Sun-Times.

Royko, wh...

and of interfering with a contract.

The Sun-Times contended that a restrictive covenant in Royko's five-year, $1.325 million contract prohibited him from working for The Tribune until two years after the personal-service contract expired on Jan. 31, 1988. The suit, which named Royko and The Tribune as defendants, also asked for an unspecified sum in money damages.

Through their attorneys, Royko and The Tribune argued on three fronts. They maintained that the personal-service contract, which they said Royko negotiated without an attorney, was not transferable to the new ownership; that the restrictive covenant was so broad as to be unenforceable because it excluded Royko from working for any newspaper that was available for purchase in Chicago; and that a so-called "escape hatch" provision in the Sun-Times contract with the Chicago Newspaper Guild took precedence over Royko's personal-service contract.

SCOTILLO SAID it was unnecessary to rule on whether Royko's contract was "assignable" to the new ownership and ruled in favor of The Tribune and Royko on the remaining two questions.

Scotillo said the covenant that prohibited Royko from writing "for any newspaper syndicate or publication which is distributed in the Chicago metropolitan newspaper market" was "unenforceable and void" under Illinois law because it was overly broad.

"It would severely limit the area in which defendant Royko could seek employment," Scotillo said in rejecting arguments from Richmond that the clause was intended to be directed at the Sun-Times' chief competitor, The Tribune.

Scotillo also said in his oral ruling that the "escape hatch" provision in the Sun-Times contract allowing guild employees to quit with full severance pay upon a change in the newspaper's ownership also covers Royko, who is a guild member.

THERE WAS NO provision in Royko's personal-service contract that was "consistent" with the general...

always. One night, Kogan recalls, "Mike had won second prize in the Bowling Writers of America contest, or some damn thing. I'm sure he never even entered—they'd just spotted some column he'd written on bowling. But the prize was a suitcase with two bowling balls in it. It sort of jutted out at awkward angles. That night he had me carry it around."

They took it into the Acorn on Oak. "I thought it was so cool," Kogan recalls. "It looked like it had two heads in there, with a space in the middle for shoes. Everyone in the bar wanted to know what it was. Mike said, 'I won this contest.' He was very proud of it." After a round of drinks, inspiration struck. Royko and Kogan got ten people to stand by the door to the bathroom like human bowling pins and proceeded to have a bowling contest in the Acorn on Oak. "We didn't bowl hard. We said, 'If it touches you, fall the way you would if you were pushed.' The people were all sort of into it."

But Royko was ready for a change, and it came in the person of an attractive and athletic blonde woman named Judy Arndt. A native of Rock Island, Illinois, Arndt came to Chicago in 1972 after spending four years in Washington working as a congressional aide and for Common Cause. She worked as a tennis pro at indoor clubs in the city until the blizzard of 1979—the one that sank Michael Bilandic—also sank the roof at the Lake Shore Club. Arndt landed at the *Sun-Times* as assistant manager of its public service bureau, which gave tours of the paper, handled requests for photos, and conducted community functions in the paper's name.

One of Arndt's first duties in the public service bureau was to handle a deluge of requests for a story that appeared in the *Sun-Times* in July of 1981. "We were there night after night," Arndt recalls, "filling requests for reprints. There was just a tremendous outpouring of reaction to that column."

It was Mike Royko's column on the eve of the wedding of Prince Charles and Diana. It was a deeply moving piece. Royko later said he'd filed a different column, went down to the Billy Goat for a drink, and had a conversation with a cynic who said the royal marriage was being arranged for some ill gain. Royko finished his drink, went back upstairs, and typed out a lovely column that spoke mostly of what two people, if they have some luck and appreciate one another, can share over the years. It was a column about love—not at first sight, but at five thousandth sight.

For all of his reputation, well earned, as a tough guy in print, a man who wrote with his fists, Royko's tender columns may have made the most lasting impression on

The great Buddy Charles.

people. One from the sixties, about a modern-day Mary and Joseph wandering the streets of Chicago on Christmas Eve, was reprinted around the world and quoted by religious leaders. There were the columns after Carol's death, and another when Royko had the sad task of eulo-

gizing John Belushi, the gifted Chicago comic whom Royko had known since Belushi was a boy. John had played a Royko-like columnist in the movie *Continental Divide*. After its Chicago premiere, a *Rolling Stone* reporter caught them in a big bear hug. Royko said he felt like a proud uncle.

Judy Arndt had read the Charles and Di column, and she had met Royko on a few work-related occasions and liked and admired him, though the admiration was tested at the first Ribfest, which Judy had helped promote, when she witnessed Royko autographing a young woman's bare midriff. "I thought: 'This is the Pulitzer Prize–winner?' I had him up on a pretty high plane."

It wasn't much later, in 1982, when Arndt was walking at the *Sun-Times* with a close friend, Chicago journalist Rick Soll, then a *Sun-Times* feature writer. As they passed the newsroom, Soll said, "I know someone who

wants to go out with you." Arndt, who had just broken off a four-year relationship with a tennis pro, said somewhat warily, "Yeah, who?"

Soll said, "Mike Royko."

"I can still remember," Arndt said later. "I stopped, and I had this view into the newsroom, and I stood there." Soll didn't need more than that—the date was arranged.

They met for dinner at a North Side hotel with a few other people in the group. Royko distinguished himself by arriving forty-five minutes late and then talking all through dinner. "I remember looking at him," Arndt says, "and thinking, 'What am I doing here?' This guy would not stop talking."

Probably nerves. At the end of dinner, the others discreetly slipped away, and Mike and Judy went to a bar next door for a drink. This time the talk was real, good enough that they repaired to the Acorn on Oak to listen to Buddy Charles. When Judy dropped him at the Lake Shore Drive condo, she watched him walk to the door. "He clicked his heels walking down the sidewalk."

She was charmed. "I thought, 'What a full-of-life person. What a good person.' I was very impressed with him right off the bat. I didn't necessarily expect to see a lot of him."

They saw each other the very next night. Royko called

John Belushi (left) in *Animal House*.

Royko once said he thought one in four of his columns was good enough to be collected in book form. His widow, Judy, brought out another, *One More Time,* in the spring of 1999. It received great reviews and went into multiple printings.

and they ended up going to see a Peter O'Toole movie, *My Favorite Year*.

"But it progressed slowly," Arndt says. Usually they went out for dinner. By late 1982 it was a couple of nights a week, and when Royko returned from his annual Florida vacation that winter, "we were pretty much inseparable."

By May of 1983 Arndt had moved into the Lake Shore Drive condo and they were talking of marriage. It was all a little fast. Judy moved out for a time, though they still saw each other, and then Royko went out to San Francisco to cover the 1984 Democratic Convention. Toward the end Judy flew out and they wound up spending a week in Carmel, one of the most breathtaking locales in the world. "It was magical," Arndt recalls. "That week was the turning point."

Royko suggested eloping in January of 1985, but they waited until April and were married in the Lake Shore condominium, with a party afterward at the Ridgemoor Country Club. Arndt saw the side of him few did, the cultured, layered, sophisticated man who, when asked by the *Tribune* food editor his favorite aphrodisiac, for a Valentine's Day feature, quoted Rostand: "A grape, a glass of water, and a half a macaroon." He taught her golf and she taught him tennis: "He was a crafty player. His mobility was not as great

as he might have hoped at that time, but he made up for it with his thinking."

One night in a restaurant Mike brought up the subject of kids. His boys were grown, Judy didn't have any, what did she think? "I hadn't had the urge to have kids before," she says. But they talked about it and their son Sam was born in 1987, and their daughter Kate, in 1992. Like more than one man before him, Royko was better equipped for fatherhood the second time around. "He was totally devoted to the kids," Judy says. He bought Sam his own bowling ball and took him to a live Power Rangers show that produced a hilarious column in which Royko recounted getting out of his seat to dance with the Putty, the bad guys in the show. Another time the columnist was

Mike and Judy

Judy, Mike, Kate, and Sam.
Royko was a better father the
second time around.

tipped that Michael Jordan would be playing golf at a
Chicago club. He took Sam out onto the back nine where
they pretended to fish in a pond, and when Jordan's
group reached a nearby tee, Royko asked for an autograph. "It's for the boy," he said, and Jordan obliged.
That moment was harder for Royko than facing down
U.S. presidents upset about a column.

He and Judy moved to Sauganash, across the Edens
Expressway from Edgebrook, and eventually out of
the city altogether, to Winnetka, a lovely northeast-
ern suburb where they found an elegant home with front
and back swings, a backyard where deer nibbled the
foliage and the kids could play, and a third floor that
Royko converted into an office. "Sam's schooling wasn't
working out," Judy said. "That was the catalyst. It was a
very big move for us to make as fast as we did. We both
loved the city. But we just did it. We found this place and
just loved it. We felt ready for a change."

Royko cut down to four columns a week and worked
on a detective novel set in Palm Springs, where he and
Judy had vacationed. He was conquering a lifelong fear of
flying. He had tried acupuncture, therapists, and a lot of
Valiums before take-off. His friend Dan Hurley, who had
Royko down to his place in Florida, remembers a story of
Royko getting on the plane at O'Hare and promptly falling

asleep. He woke a couple of hours later, checked his watch, and said to Judy, "Wonderful. We're here."

"No," she replied. "We haven't taken off. We've been sitting here for two hours. The plane has a mechanical problem."

Eventually the country's poor passenger-train service got to him enough that Royko became serious about getting over his fear, and he pretty much overcame it. "It was like the world opened up to him," Judy says. "He was really excited. He'd gotten a book about all the places we could stay in Europe." Royko even bought a computer program that let him pilot a plane. "But he always crashed into the Hancock Building," Judy says. "He couldn't get around the Hancock Building, but he was working on it."

He did enjoy the computer, immersing himself in it as he did all new interests. A housekeeper once asked if she could use the computer the following morning for a personal project. Royko said sure, and that night he played with it for a while. When the housekeeper turned it on the next day, she was soon frowning and looking over her shoulder. The computer was belching. "She had no idea what was going on," Judy recalls. "It belched—loud—every twenty seconds or so."

In some ways, things had never been better. He loved his new family, and he was getting closer to his older boys and their families as well. There was a Mike Royko Day at Wrigley Field. He had become a key figure in the Chicago landscape, outlasting his detractors with a singular talent and work ethic drawn from his milkman father all those years ago. He was friendly with the new Chicago mayor, Richard M. Daley, son of Royko's old adversary, and the powerful Tribune Media Services was syndicating his column, which meant papers could buy it individually, rather than as part of a package. His audience grew staggeringly large, with the column in over 600 papers in the 1980s and 1990s.

There were interview requests from all over, and he consented to a few, often expressing amazement at his own longevity and wonder at where the years had gone.

On the thirtieth anniversary of the column, in 1994, Royko granted a long interview to Chris Robling of WBEZ public radio in Chicago. It took place in Royko's third-floor home office and Robling was nervous, at least until his host cracked open a six-pack of Coors and said fire away. Robling's first question was how Royko felt about the anniversary.

"I'm tired," he said, and laughed. "When the *Tribune* reminded me I've been doing it thirty years—because I don't keep track—I was kind of surprised. It doesn't seem like thirty years. What's strange is that I'll be talking to my assistant, and I'll mention the '68 Convention, and I'll get kind of a blank look. Because I think she was born in '68. That's when I realize how long I've been doing the thing."

He laughed when he told Robling he was tired—but he *was* tired. Given the standard he set for himself, punching out a column day after day for decades would have worn down anyone, and then, too, Royko was tired of the suits at the *Tribune* who seemed to notice him only when he got in trouble. The *Daily News* had been home. The *Tribune* was a job. He was weary as well of changes creeping into the newspaper business, where an unstated but nevertheless understood insistence that you write a certain way and never, above all else, *offend*

anyone or any group, was the new orthodoxy. Royko fumed. Where in the Constitution did it say people have the right not to be offended? After Royko's death, the journalist who succeeded Royko on page three of the *Tribune,* John Kass, said of his predecessor: "How do you write well and not offend people? What are we supposed to do? Give people oatmeal?"

Royko would not. Asked by Robling if the armies of political correctness were taking away his ability to use the language, Royko said, "They're trying their darnedest. They're not going to do it to me because I'm at a point in my life and career where, no, you're not going to do this to me. Squawk all you want, picket me, I don't care. I will say what I want to say the way I want to say it."

Within a year of the Robling interview, Royko would be embroiled in controversies that were among the toughest of his career. First there was a drunk driving bust in Winnetka during which the columnist conversed with the arresting officers in language that no one would have deemed politically correct. The police reports leaked, and the *Wall Street Journal* used the occasion to run an unflattering front-page profile of Royko that intimated he was a dinosaur that had stayed

Shedding light on Wrigley Field

Mike Royko JAN 84

NOW THAT THE ALIEN has been repelled, let's get on to more important matters.

While taking a walk in my neighborhood, I ran into a friend who lives a short distance from Wrigley Field.

He tends to be cynical, so I wasn't surprised when he said:

"Now that you're on their payroll, I guess we've lost you, right?"

He didn't have to explain what he was talking about. What he meant was the following:

1. He's against lights in Wrigley Field because he thinks the crowds for night baseball will screw up his neighborhood.

2. The Cubs and the ballpark are owned by the Tribune Co.

3. So is this paper.

4. I used to be against lights in Wrigley Field.

5. Now I'm on the Trib payroll.

6. Therefore, good company man that I am, I'm no longer against lights in Wrigley Field.

7. So I'm a fink.

WE MIGHT AS well clear that up now.

My opinion on lights hasn't changed. I'm against night games in Wrigley Field unless it can be proved, to the satisfaction of the majority of the people who live nearby, that the neighborhood won't be hurt.

It's not that I wouldn't enjoy night games. As a fan, I would. I can walk to the ballpark from my home, so after a day's work I wouldn't mind strolling over and getting a few laughs out of the high comedy of the Cubs.

It could also be therapeutic. Sometimes I have a deep sense of guilt at how much money I'm paid for doing so little. I've even thought of going to a shrink and telling him about those guilt feelings.

But when these feelings hit me, it would be much cheaper to go watch the Cubs, and when I see one of them flailing his bat at the air or catching a ball with his brow, I could tell myself: "Me and those million-dollar clowns work for the same outfit. And I think I'm overpaid?"

THEN I COULD go home to bed with a clear conscience.

And there's another consideration. Cheering for the Cubs, or laughing, causes a parchness of the throat, requiring a constant flow of liquid.

When a game has ended, I've sometimes found myself

Mike Royko 3-12-84 TRIB.

...ts mistakes ...P for GOD

...ELL something was wrong. President ...een on the TV at the end of the bar ...But Slats Grobnik hadn't said even ...its hoots, jeers, snorts, hisses or ...to his nose and wiggles his bony ...publican—especially a Republi...

..."That's why I love TV. My ...ame advance, just like me. ...rs and radio in his day. There was ...ch fun thumbing your nose ...radio did." ...olitely glancing at his home ...y at the TV screen, I ...shed him if something

...g somebody, then ...to do with my soul."

...g what I ... you do? ... it a ...

Bobbitt hit belo...

...uring t... ...one of t... subject ... "I've ... Bobbit... hear it?"...

Despite my p... for a lunch con... to go on. So he... Big John wa... Had a wife u... One night w... With a knif... As a lowe... To my disa... laughed. But... sensitive.

Even wors... began comp... ...ding alou...

Sometimes I have a deep sense of guilt at how much money I'm paid for doing so little. I've even thought of going to a shrink and telling him about these guilt feelings. But when these feelings hit me, it would be much cheaper to go watch the Cubs, and when I see one of them flailing his bat at the air or catching a ball with his brow, I could tell myself: "Me and those million-dollar clowns work for the same outfit. And I think I'm overpaid?" Then I could go home to bed with a clear conscience.

Top *Left to right,* Dave, Rob, and Mike Royko.

Middle **Relaxing on vacation in Florida.**

Bottom **On vacation with Kate and Sam.**

past its time. Lois Wille, Royko's longtime colleague and staunch friend, told the paper, "He hasn't changed. But I think people's sensitivities have."

There was an irony at work. What Royko was doing in the 1990s was challenging the power structure, questioning assumptions, deflating egos, and pointing out absurdities. He was, above all, calling it as he saw it. He had done so to great acclaim throughout his career and he wasn't about to stop because some of the groups and individuals he felt compelled to criticize weren't Irish males who smoked cigars. But despite his thirty-year track record of sticking up for the underdog, people sometimes forgot. After the drunk driving arrest, he wrote a satirical column about Mexico's problems with drugs and illegal emigration that brought thousands of Hispanics into the street in front of Tribune Tower in protest.

"They don't remember," Kass said. "In my neighborhood, say the corner of Fifty-fifth and California, if Royko had come into those neighborhoods after writing about open-housing discrimination in the '60s—when it counted, when it was real, and the tensions were right there and he stood up to it—there wouldn't have been a protest. They would have grabbed him by the ankles and tried to beat him up. People either conveniently forgot or pretended to forget in order to build up a political case against him."

Some friends thought that the move to Winnetka,

as wonderful as it was in many ways, as good for the family as it must have been, hurt his ability to bounce controversial columns off trusted colleagues. It was also not impossible that he had lost a step. Thirty years is a very long time on the high wire, and by then his health wasn't the best. He was taking pills for high blood pressure and doctors were pressuring him to have angioplasty, which he eventually did. "He just didn't feel well," Judy Royko said.

His longtime associate Hanke Gratteau saw in some isolated instances an imprecision in his writing that had not been present before.

"The wonderful thing about Mike's satiric side," Gratteau says, "is he could walk right to the line, but he was always on the right side of the line. If you read [the Mexico column], it's going along fine and it's right there at the line, but there's a couple of paragraphs where it crosses into some mean-spiritedness, where it's propelled over the line."

According to Gratteau, Royko was deeply hurt by the reaction to the column. Rick Kogan concurs: "I think what bummed him out was the lack of support from a few old friends and from some people at the paper he worked for."

"Mike was deeply hurt," Gratteau says, "and never wavered for an instant in his belief he'd never crossed the line. And I sat there with him a couple of times when I was very uncomfortable, and we had one of the most uncomfortable moments of our relationship because I could not chime in, 'You're right. I have no idea what they're talking about.' It was horrible, because he wanted me to say it, and I couldn't. There was absolutely nothing, ever, in the man's heart, that was racist or mean-spirited. But there was an imprecision in that writing that I felt I had never seen before."

It was as hard on him as just about anything had been. "I saw him with tears of frustration over the abuse he took," Gratteau recalls. "People not remembering, not viewing it against the body of his lifelong work."

Kogan thinks it was Royko's own consideration of that career that helped him move past the controversy. "He knew who he was. He had been in bigger fights."

He was helped, too, by a few weeks passing and the lynch mob setting its sights on someone else, maybe a golfer or a baseball manager who told a stupid joke and now found his entire career in jeopardy. And of course he was helped by his sense of humor.

"I think liberals have good hearts," Royko had said a year or two earlier in an interview. "I can never really get that mad at liberals, because they're so warm-hearted. They really want everybody to be happy. They want everything to be just right. Except it's never going to happen.

Despite his usual casual appearance, Royko could look pretty snappy in a tux as evidenced here on his and Judy's wedding day.

Everything isn't going to be just right. Everybody isn't going to be happy. And if you really try to remake the whole society to make everything right, you're going to screw it up worse than it is now. . . . If a guy is really short, and I can't call him short, he ain't gonna get any taller. I don't want to refer to people in a derogatory way. But let's be realistic about it. I guess I'm follicle-challenged. Don't call me bald! I don't think most people think that way."

Though the controversies got the most attention, Royko in fact did some of his best work in the 1990s, columns on national issues that were taped on refrigerators from coast to coast. The awards didn't stop, either. In 1990 Royko received the National Press Club's annual Fourth Estate Award for exemplifying the highest principles of journalism, and in 1995 he received the Denver Press Club's Damon Runyon Award for lifelong excellence in news reporting.

In a 1991 column Royko ridiculed Los Angeles Police Chief Daryl Gates for suggesting that Rodney King might benefit in the long run from the beating by police. A few years later, in what could almost have been a companion piece, at the start of the O. J. Simpson trial, Royko wrote a dead-on column predicting that Simpson would walk, even explaining why. Black jurors who had themselves been victimized by police would not vote to convict him.

With his fear of flying largely conquered, Mike and Judy bought a condominium on Long Boat Key in Sarasota, Florida. It was a splendid location. He could walk out the back door and be fifty yards from the beach.

He talked with Hurley about maybe quitting the column. He had said it before, though, and who knew? As John Sciackitano had said some years before, "He needs to be Mike Royko, and Mike Royko writes five columns a week." But he had cut back to four—to the delight of Judy, since it meant he actually had a weekend—and now he seemed serious telling Hurley he might have had enough.

"He was seriously thinking of going to three days a week," Hurley recalls. "He talked about going for another two years and then retiring. He was going to go to Ireland and get the big mansion, and there would be a little cottage for me. I would have to refer to him as 'Squire.' He was going to teach me to fish."

They never got to Ireland. In the early spring of 1997, Mike and Judy and the kids went to Longboat Key. Mike's last column before the vacation was a winner. With baseball season approaching he addressed the supposed curse Billy Goat founder William Sianis had put on the Cubs for barring his goat from Wrigley Field in the 1940s. A good story, Royko allowed, but utter nonsense. The Cubs were actually cursed by ownership that for too many years was reluctant to hire black ballplayers. If a goat was to blame, the goat was wearing a gabardine suit and sitting behind an executive's desk.

About the time Mike and Judy left for Florida, Bob and Geri Royko had just returned home from their own vacation in the Florida Keys when they got a phone call that Mike had taken ill.

They flew back to Florida, landing in Tampa where they were told Mike had been transferred from Sarasota Memorial Hospital to a hospital in Gainesville, which had one of the preeminent brain specialists in the country. Mike had an aneurysm.

Bob and Geri waited in Tampa and were joined by Mike's son David. The three of them drove to Long Boat Key, where Judy's sister, Connie, was watching Sam and Kate. Judy was with Mike at the hospital in Gainesville.

After a couple of days Judy called and told them to come to Gainesville. When they arrived, Mike was in good spirits, lucid and ready for surgery. The procedure was deemed a success. "Bob, David, and I saw Mike the following day," Geri recalls. "Although he was sedated, he looked great and was raising all kinds of hell in the ICU recovery room."

Everyone was cautiously optimistic. The *Tribune* sent a plane for Mike and Judy, and Mike was checked into Rush Presbyterian Hospital in Chicago. He was not, we can be certain, the most mild-mannered patient. Soon Royko was allowed to go home, and after a few days he was insisting on being allowed to climb the stairs to his third-floor office. On April 22 he had another, more serious brain episode and collapsed. It took some time for the ambulance to arrive. He was transported to Northwestern Memorial Hospital and placed on life support. The family had time to say goodbye. He died on April 29, 1997.

Almost two years later, Judy Royko would say, "He sometimes said he thought he would be like Nelson Algren, who he felt was never properly appreciated after his death."

That didn't happen. Mike Royko is appreciated. The outpouring of grief and sympathy in the days and weeks after his death was tremendous. Just before Royko's death, his friend and colleague Jim Warren wrote a piece about small-town newspaper editors around the country who had said how much having Royko's column in their paper meant to them. Warren quoted Jack Moseley, editor of the *Southwest Times Record* of Fort Smith, Arkansas. "He's like the people who live here," Moseley said. "He gets hacked off at stupidity. He has a temper and seems to care about the little guy who gets screwed."

Janet McMillan, editor of the *Daily Journal* in Vineland, New Jersey, recalled the reaction when her predecessor had dropped Royko: "As soon as I got here, I started getting unsolicited calls. People wanted him back. They had a feeling he was speaking for the average guy.

up with both barrels. I didn't like it, but I haven't missed a vote since."

In Chicago, TV and radio shows were full of tributes. The *Tribune* ran an entire special section devoted to Royko, and the paper's Web site overflowed with people's remembrances. It was overwhelming. Six weeks after his death, Geri Royko said, "I don't think Michael knew how much people loved him." Columnists around the world of all creeds, colors, and genders wrote appreciations. Many said it was because of Mike Royko that they got into the business of journalism.

In June of 1997, on a hot, sunny day in Chicago, Studs Terkel hosted a memorial service at Wrigley Field, and Harry Caray sang—what else?—"Take Me Out to the Ball Game." Bob Royko spoke about his brother, John Sciackitano remembered his great friend, Ellen Warren spoke for the leg people, and Dave Royko read some of his dad's letters to Carol from the 1950s. There was music—Rob Royko played guitar, Mike's niece Amelia, a promising singer, performed, and Buddy Charles played his matchless piano.

A grove of trees in Lincoln Park was named in his

You have all these fancy writers and great political analysts out there, but just one Royko. That's why I got him back."

In Royko's *New York Times* obituary, the Reverend Jesse Jackson called him "an equal opportunity shot taker." Jackson recalled working in California in 1972 to get out the vote, preaching that every vote counted but being too exhausted to return to Chicago and vote himself. "It was contradictory to what I had been saying," Jackson laughed. "Somehow Royko found out about it and opened

honor, and in March of 1999 *Chicago* magazine ranked Royko among the 25 Most Important Chicagoans of the Twentieth Century. In April Judy Royko and the University of Chicago Press brought out a definitive collection of Mike's columns, *One More Time,* with an introduction by Terkel and annotations by Lois Wille.

Chicago is still Chicago. Politics and sports still dominate the barroom talk. But something is missing. "When nature removes a great man," Ralph Waldo Emerson wrote, "people explore the horizon for a successor; but none comes, and none will. His class is extinguished with him."

But if you listen closely around Chicago and elsewhere, in elevators and on sidewalks, occasionally you'll hear a new version of Chicagoans' phrase of thirty-five years ago—"Ju-read-Royko?" It's a bit different now. "What would he say about Y2K? About Viagra? About Monica Lewinsky? What would Mike Royko say?"

He would say it best.

Honors and Awards

1963–1978

Chicago Daily News
Reporter, columnist

1968 *Heywood Broun Award*
The award was for his coverage of the 1968
Democratic National Convention.
1971 *National Headliner Award*
1972 *Pulitzer Prize* (for commentary)

1978–1983

Chicago Sun-Times
Reporter, columnist

1980 Named to the Chicago Journalism Hall
of Fame
1981 *H. L. Mencken Award*
Presented by the *Baltimore Sun* newspapers,
the award honors the nation's top reporter
whose intellect and prose are in the tradition of the iconoclast.
1982 *Ernie Pyle Award*
Named for the World War II correspondent,
the award recognized Royko for outstanding
human interest reporting.

1984–1997

Chicago Tribune
Columnist

1990 *National Press Club's Annual Fourth
Estate Award*
Presented to Royko for exemplifying the
highest principles of journalism.
1995 *Denver Press Club's Damon Runyon
Award*
Presented to Royko for lifelong excellence in
news reporting.

Bibliography

Books

Blei, Norbert. *Chi Town*. Granite Falls, Minn.: Ellis Press, 1990.

Breslin, Jimmy. *I Want to Thank My Brain for Remembering Me*. Boston: Little, Brown, 1996.

Ciccone, F. Richard. *Chicago and the American Century*. Chicago: Contemporary Books, 1999.

Dornfeld, A. A. *Behind the Front Page: The Story of the City News Bureau of Chicago*. Chicago: Academy Chicago, 1983.

Grauer, Neil. *Wits and Sages*. Baltimore: Johns Hopkins University Press, 1984.

Kelley, Kitty. *His Way: The Unauthorized Biography of Frank Sinatra*. New York: Bantam, 1986.

Royko, Mike. *Boss: Richard J. Daley of Chicago*. New York: Dutton, 1971.

Articles

Brashler, William. "The Man Who Owns Chicago." *Esquire,* May 8, 1979.

Coburn, Marcia Froelke. "Says Who? Says He!" *Chicago,* March 1990.

Crimmins, Jerry, and Rick Kogan. "Newspaper Legend Mike Royko Dies." *Chicago Tribune,* April 30, 1997.

Duff, Christina. "Has a Curmudgeon Turned into a Bully? Some Now Think So." *Wall Street Journal,* July 20, 1995.

Ebert, Roger. "Film Critic Roger Ebert Recalls Royko as a Friend and Guide to Chicago." *Chicago Sun-Times,* April 30, 1997.

Eig, Jonathan. "The Last Word." *Chicago,* October 1997.

Greene, Bob. "Like Playing on a Diamond with DiMaggio." *Chicago Tribune,* May 4, 1997.

Holder, Dennis. "Mike Royko." *Washington Journalism Review,* June 1981.

Schulian, John. "Slug It: Royko." *GQ,* March 1985.

Terry, Don. "Mike Royko, the Voice of the Working Class, Dies at 64." *New York Times,* April 30, 1997.

Tuohy, James. "Real Royko." *New City,* May 1997.

Warren, James. "In Towns Across Nation, Mike Royko Is Legendary." *Chicago Tribune,* April 27, 1997.

Wills, Garry. "In Cold Type." *Vanity Fair,* May 1984.

Credits and Permissions

Pages 77, 97
Wisconsin Center for Film and Theater
Research

Pages 80, 81
Photos courtesy of Hanke Gratteau

Page 95
Tribune Tower photo © Jeff Scott Olson;
news story, *Chicago Tribune*; photo of news
story © Jeff Scott Olson

Page 96
Photo courtesy of the Drake Hotel

Page 98
Photo of books © Jeff Scott Olson

Page 100
Courtesy of the Royko family; photo by
Karen Rodgers Photography

Page 102
Column, *Chicago Tribune*; photo of column
© Jeff Scott Olson